How to Awaken Your True Potential

How to Awaken Your True Potential

Paramhansa Yogananda

Crystal Clarity Publishers
Nevada City, California

Crystal Clarity Publishers, Nevada City, CA 95959

Paperback ISBN: 978-1-56589-298-9
ePub ISBN: 978-1-56589-559-1

Printed in China
1 3 5 7 9 10 8 6 4 2

Cover and interior design by Tejindra Scott Tully

LIBRARY OF CONGRESS CATALOGING-IN-PUBLICATION DATA

Yogananda, Paramahansa, 1893-1952.

How to awaken your true potential / Paramhansa Yogananda.
-- 1st [edition]. pages cm

ISBN 978-1-56589-298-9 (quality pbk. : alk. paper) --
ISBN 978-1-56589-559-1 (epub)

1. Self-realization--Religious aspects--Self-Realization Fellowship. I. Title.

BP605.S4Y5439 2016
294.5'44--dc23

2015033132

www.crystalclarity.com
clarity@crystalclarity.com
800-424-1055

Contents

How to Awaken Your True Potential

Chapter *1*

A Sacred Invitation

COME OUT of your closed chamber of limitation. Breathe in the fresh air of vital thoughts. Exhale poisonous thoughts of discouragement, discontentment, or hopelessness. Never suggest to your mind human limitations of sickness, old age, or death, but constantly remind yourself, "I am the Infinite, which has become the body."

Take long mental walks on the path of self-confidence. Exercise with instruments of judgment, introspection, and initiative. Feast unstintingly on creative thinking within yourself and others.

Above all, cultivate the habit of meditation. This is the inner switch you turn on to connect yourself with the Infinite. Hold on to the after-effects of meditation by your attention. You will then find that you are a reservoir of power in body, mind, and soul. By constantly holding in mind the peaceful after-effects of meditation, by feeling immortality in the body, and by feeling the ocean of God's bliss beneath the changeable waves of experiences, the soul can find perpetual rejuvenation.

You are all gods, if you only knew it. You must look within. Behind the wave of your consciousness is the sea of God's presence. Claim your Divine Birthright. Awake, and you shall behold the glory of God.

—*Paramhansa Yogananda*

Dear Reader,

Paramhansa Yogananda offers a vision of who you are in truth. By following his wise counsel, you can free yourself from limiting thoughts and behaviors, and discover the freedom and bliss that await you in the inner stillness of your own being.

Meditation is widely recommended today by experts in many fields, from health professionals to sports heroes. Yogananda introduces you to meditation and helps you discover its enormous potential. You'll learn how meditation can take you beyond stress-free living, beyond even inner peace, to the realization of your own highest self, your true potential.

Yogananda's words, potent with soul inspiration, guide you through the essential steps to free yourself from limitations: to transform your daily habits, to discover the power of your mind, to use meditation to experience your true nature, and, finally, to make your outward life a reflection of your ever-expanding awareness.

As Yogananda loved to say: "The time for knowing God has come!"

—*Crystal Clarity Publishers*

Chapter 2

Control Your Destiny

→1←

Whatever you have made yourself in the past, that is what you are now. By the secret, invisible traces of your own past actions, you have been controlling the power of your present actions.

Through the law of cause and effect that governs actions, you have ordered yourself to be punished or rewarded. You have probably suffered enough. It is time now for you to parole yourself from the prison of your own past undesirable habits. Since you are the judge, if you are ready to liberate yourself, no jail of suffering, poverty, or ignorance can hold you.

→2←

If failures invade you repeatedly, don't get discouraged. They should act as stimulants and not poisons to your material or spiritual growth. The period of failure is the best season for sowing the seeds of success. Weed out the causes of failure, and launch with double vigor what you want to accomplish. The bludgeon of circumstances may bleed you, but keep your head unbowed.

Death in the attempt to succeed is success; refuse to harbor the consciousness of defeat. Try always once more, no matter how many times you have failed. Persevere one minute more in the race for success when you have done your best and think you can do no more.

To illustrate: *A* and *B* were boxing for a prize. *A* thought, "I have punched and punched, and I cannot go on." *B* thought the same thing. But then *A* thought, "I can give just one more punch." So *A* made one more effort, and down went *B*. That is what you must do. Just give *one more punch*.

3

Habit is an automatic mental mechanism for performing actions without the will power and effort involved in initiating new actions. Habits make the performance of actions easier. Good habits and virtues are eternal joy-making qualities.

Wrongly used, this mechanism becomes man's archenemy. Bad habits attract evil things. Bad habits and sin are temporary misery-making grafts on the soul.

It is lamentable to be compelled to do evil against one's will because of the strength of an evil habit, and then to have to suffer for one's evil actions. It is wonderful to habitually do what is right and thus multiply goodness and happiness.

The power of habit is supreme in the life of man. Most people spend their lives making good mental resolutions, but never succeed in following what is wholesome. We usually do not do what we wish to do, but only what we are accustomed to do.

Do not feel helpless if you have some undesirable habits. Now is the time to begin conquering them by developing will power and the habit of regular, right meditation. You can free yourself from the clutches of wrong habits and create habits of thought and action that will bring the results you desire.

→4←

If you haven't enough will power, try to develop "won't" power. When you are at the dinner table and Mr. Greed tries to chloroform your self-control and lure you to eat more than you should, watch yourself. After partaking of the right quality and quantity of food, say to yourself, "I won't eat any more," and get up from the table and run. When somebody calls: "John, come back. Don't forget the delicious apple pie," just call back, "I won't."

5

The only way to avoid temptation is to know that there are higher things than temptation. When temptation comes, *first* stop the action or the force. When the temptation is gone, *then* reason, for temptation will overcome all reason. Just say "No," and get up and go. That is the surest way to destroy temptation. The more you develop this "won't" power during the advent of temptation, the happier you will be, because happiness depends upon the ability to do things you should do.

Habit sits like an octopus in the brain and commands you to do a certain thing. You don't want to do that thing and yet you do it. Never let yourself reach the point where you find yourself a victim of wrong habits. Remember that you must be the boss of yourself. Do not let anything or anyone run you. If anything undesirable becomes a habit with you, it is time to stop it.

As a rule, I do not like commandments. Whenever you command someone not to do a certain thing, that person seems determined to do it. The taste of forbidden fruit is sweet in the beginning, but bitter in the end. You should be very careful not to let anything interfere with your happiness.

⇾6⇽

The Man Who Thought He Was Proof Against Temptation

Mr. J. was a confirmed drunkard. After meeting a saint, he took a vow to abstain from drinking. He asked his servants to hide his costly wine in locked boxes, to keep the key, and to serve the liquor only to his friends. For some time Mr. J. felt joy in the power of his new resolution against drink. He was unaware of the unseen gripping lure of the liquor habit.

As time went on and he felt himself proof against liquor temptation, he asked his servants to leave the key to the wine room with him so that he could serve his friends himself. Feeling mental security, he decided it was too much bother to go to the cellar to get liquor for his friends, so he kept some wine bottles hidden in the parlor. After a few days, Mr. J. thought: "Since I am proof against liquor, let me enjoy the sparkling red wine in the bottle on the table."

Every day he looked at the bottle. Then he thought: "Since I no longer care for liquor, I will take a taste of the wine, and spit it out." He did this. Then he thought: "Since I am so strong in my resolve, there will be no harm if I swallow just a sip." After that, he thought: "Since I have conquered the liquor habit, let me take only one gulp of wine at a time, as many times as my un-enslaved will desires." Then he got drunk and kept on being helplessly drunk every day, just as he had before, in spite of his resolve.

Mr. J. failed to realize that his resolution against liquor had not had time to ripen into a good habit. It takes from five to eight years to substitute a good habit for a strong bad habit. Before the strong good habit is formed, the devotee must stay away from evil habit-forming environments or actions. Above all, he must never let evil thoughts enter the mind. The thoughts cause the actions and are therefore more dangerous.

If you have a tendency to live on the misery-producing material plane, learn to stay away from tempting environments and to cast out thoughts of temptation. Surround yourself with the right environment, and keep your mind filled with thoughts that benefit you.

7

One cause of failure is that you do not weigh your bad habits against the power of free will required to combat them. Extraordinary talent is not as necessary as unswerving purpose and unfailing effort. Do not continue to carry your burden of old mental and moral weaknesses from the past, but burn them in the fires of resolution and become free.

When you determine to do something that you know is absolutely right, go through with it at any cost. This will give your wisdom-guided will more power over your bad habits. Renounce last year's material failure, mental and moral weaknesses, spiritual indifference, and half-hearted meditations by using your will to be prosperous, to exercise self-control, and to meditate deeply until you actually contact God.

In meditation, the mind withdraws the life force from the muscles and nerves, and concentrates it in the brain cells, where the evil mental habits are grooved. This concentrated life energy in the brain burns out the grooves of mental habits lodged there.

The right method of meditation is the only way to all-round freedom and lasting success. You must consciously contact God. Finding Him, you will attain dominion over yourself and all limiting conditions.

Chapter 3

Choose Freedom, Not Misery

→1←

Only by the fire of persistent effort can malignant seeds of past karma be roasted and destroyed. Most people give up hope just when the balance of good karma slowly stoops toward them to give fruit, and thus they miss their reward.

→2←

Idleness is extremely detrimental to spiritual realization. Laziness in body or mind must be driven away before you can emerge to the kingdom of God. As soldiers on the battlefield must never know idleness, so the spiritual man must be absolutely free from mental or physical idleness.

Never let yourself think that work is too much for you. Remember that God is creating universes and He is never tired; if we want to be like Him, we must have His tremendous capacity for activity.

Whatever you are doing, always think that you are doing God's work. Each day, say, "What can I do for God today?" Do your best today and forget tomorrow. Do not harass the soul with petty worries. God will take care of everything.

→3←

Your engagement with business is important, but your appointment with serving others is more important, and your engagement with meditation, God, and Truth is most important. Don't say you are too busy keeping the wolf from the door to have time to develop heavenly qualities. Break your self-satisfied, immovable habit of idolizing your less important engagements and ignoring your most important engagement with wisdom. No one else will answer for your actions.

Engagements with Over-activity and Mr. Idleness lead to misery. It is time for the modern man to shake his drowsiness and systematize his life. The modern man has learned to apply science and system to business for his material comfort. He ought also to apply science and system to improve his health, prosperity, social life, and wisdom.

Systematize and schedule your engagements. Let the secretary of your true judgment arrange your life's daily itinerary.

→4←

Bad habits of greed, anger, envy, drinking, sloth, and failure are "elected to office" by unwise hordes of little actions, whose numerical strength alone elected them, without thought of the subsequent enslavement.

Habit-slaves are not born; they make themselves that way through their constantly repeated actions. The first drink never made a drunkard. A series of thoughtless repetitions of the wrong action elected the gripping habit as ruler. Quantitative strength won against the weak qualitative voice of reason, which had no votes because it had not been exercising its powers.

Guard yourself against the first performance of an evil action. What you do once, you are liable to do again. Like a snowball rolling downhill, habit grows bigger and stronger by repetition. Use your reason in all your actions; otherwise, you can become a helpless slave of undesirable habits.

"For whosoever hath, to him shall be given; but whosoever hath not, from him shall be taken away even that which he hath." This biblical statement is very true of habits. A man of good actions increases in virtue, but a slave of bad habits loses all power of will and reason.

Try from today to overcome the hidden enemy habits within you, and be free to act from reason alone. Your habits are not you. Be yourself, and you will remember the lost image of God within you.

→5←

Every new effort after a failure must be well planned and charged with increasing intensity of attention.

→6←

The subconscious mind is like a parrot and repeats whatever we tell it. Instead of suggesting to the mind fatigue, complaints, and troubled thoughts, suggest joy, opulence, and peace, and these things will manifest in your life.

Work willingly and untiringly; feel the eternal energy flowing in you ceaselessly. Never suggest tiredness or fatigue. Never say, "I am tired."

→7←

Once habits of the body begin to rule the mind, it becomes difficult to make the body obey the commands of mind and will. That is why chronically fat people do not easily get rid of fat even if they diet. Their body cells have formed their own habits and do not instantly respond to mental commands, as they would if they had been trained to obey the superior mental forces that have the power to rule the body properly.

→8←

Do you think you are completely shattered, whipped, lacking power? No. You have all the power you want, but you don't use it. There is nothing greater than the power of the mind. Resurrect your mind from the little habits that keep you worldly. Smile that perpetual smile—the smile of God—that billion-dollar smile that no one can take from you.

→9←

Remember, it rests with you whether you want greed, sense-slavery, anger, hatred, revengefulness, worries, or disharmonies to rule your life, or whether you will let the divine soldiers of self-control, calmness, love, forgiveness, peace, and harmony rule your mental kingdom. Drive away the rebel sense habits that have brought misery to the empire of your peace. Be a king of yourself, letting the soldiers of goodness and good habits rule the kingdom of your mind. Then happiness will reign within you forever.

10

Never count your faults. Just see that your love for God is deeply sincere. For God doesn't mind your imperfections: He minds your indifference.

11

Never mind if you have erred. Just call to God with trusting love. Hide nothing from Him. He knows all your faults, far better than you do! Be completely open with Him.

You may find it helpful to pray to God as your Divine Mother. For the Mother aspect of God is all-merciful. Pray: "Divine Mother, naughty or good, I am Thy child. Thou must release me!"

Even the human mother loves her naughty children as much as her good ones. Sometimes she loves them even more, for their need is greater.

→12←

Give to God not only the good that you do, but also the bad. I do not mean that you should deliberately do things that are wrong. But when you cannot help yourself because of too-strong habits, feel that God is acting through you. Make *Him* responsible. He likes that!

It is He, after all, who has dreamed your existence. You have merely hypnotized yourself with the thought of your weaknesses. If you make the Lord responsible for your weaknesses, it will help you break the false hold they have on your imagination. You'll find it easier, then, to recognize in yourself the perfect image of God.

As long as you are making the effort, God will *never* let you down!

CHAPTER *4*

FREE YOURSELF FROM LIMITING HABITS

➔1⟵

The Boy Who Became a Saint

In my school in India, there was a boy who was brought in by his parents. We used to take only children under twelve years of age, but he was much older. I told him he could stay on one condition—that he was willing to be good.

I had a heart-to-heart talk with him and said: "You have made up your mind to smoke, but your parents do not want you to smoke. You have succeeded in defeating your parents, but you have not succeeded in defeating your own misery. You are hurting yourself."

My arrow had struck home, and he began to weep. He said, "They are always beating me."

I said: "Think of what you are doing to yourself. Come on, I will take you, on one condition—that I will not be a detective, but your friend. As long as you are willing to correct your mistakes I will be your helper, but if you tell lies, I will do nothing for you. Lying destroys friendship. Do not lie to me."

I accepted him and said, "Anytime you want to smoke, I will get you cigarettes."

One day, he came to me and said, "I feel a terrible desire to smoke." I offered him money, and he could scarcely believe his eyes. He said, "Take back the money." He did not want it. I was pushing him to go and buy the cigarettes, but he would not go. At last, after this tug-of-war, he said, "You will not believe me, but I no longer want to smoke."

The result of all the teaching and discipline was that he finally became a saint. I roused his spiritual consciousness. The greatest of all spiritual consciousness lies in the inner effort to go upstream toward lasting happiness. Very few people are making the effort. However, you can make a constant effort to become good, even if your sins are as deep as the Atlantic Ocean. Through a few incarnations you have been a human being, but through eternity you have been a child of God.

→2←

Why think of yourself as a sinner? Oh, it may be all right sometimes, in the name of humility, provided your attention is focused on the greatness of God and not on your smallness before Him. But why dwell on negativity and limitation?

If you want to find something valuable that has been buried under a mudslide, won't you be thinking of that object even as you dig through the mud? If you concentrated only on the mud, you might lose sight of your very purpose in digging and abandon the search.

3

Oversensitivity and Self-pity

We should not be touchy or have self-pity, which increases our oversensitivity. You may be nursing a grievance about something and nobody knows what it is. It is best for you to look within yourself to remove the cause of that sensitiveness.

Many people think they should pity themselves and that self-pity will bring a little relief, but self-pity is an addiction like opium. Every time an opium addict takes the drug, he becomes more and more steeped in the habit. Be as firm as steel against self-pity.

If the fire of sensitiveness eats into your heart and you allow it to stay there, it eats into the fibers of your peace. You must be able to control it yourself, knowing that oversensitivity is an agent of Satan trying to destroy your peace. Every time sensitiveness visits your heart, it disconnects you from the divine song of peace that might play within you if you were not oversensitive. Whenever sensitiveness comes, try to conquer your emotion, and do not blame others. Take responsibility for it yourself. That is the way to get rid of it.

→4←

One who was born disadvantaged in any way should resist fiercely the temptation to wallow in self-pity. To feel sorry for oneself is to dilute one's inner power to overcome. Instead, affirm: There are *no* obstacles. There are only *opportunities*!

Accuse no one, not even yourself. Blame and accusation won't erase what has been done; it will affirm, rather, your dependency on circumstances over which, truly, you no longer have control.

Seek God in inner silence. Reconcile yourself to what *is,* and to what needs to be done about it. You can reshape every karma, provided that from today onward you live by soul-consciousness.

⇾5⇽

Sorrow

Sorrow is not overcome by sorrow but by joy. Some sorrows we like to indulge in; but do not let sorrow remain with you too long, or it will rob you of the richest of your soul's possessions—perennial bliss.

⇾6⇽

Inferiority and Superiority Complexes

An inferiority complex is just as bad as a superiority complex. Inherently, you are a child of God, so it's false to think you are inferior or superior. Both inferiority and superiority complexes retard the soul's progress.

You must feel that God is within you, guiding you, and that God is your greatest love and your greatest superior. You are the servant of all; therefore you cannot think of yourself as superior. Because God is within you, you cannot think yourself inferior.

An inferiority complex is born of contact with weak-minded people, and from having a weak innate subconscious mind. A superiority complex is born of the upstart ego and the consciousness of false pride. Both live on imagination and ignore the realm of facts. Neither belongs to the true, all-powerful soul.

Develop self-confidence by conquering your weaknesses. Found your self-confidence upon real, growing achievements, and you will be free from all inferiority and superiority complexes.

7

Fear

Fear is a mental poison, unless it is used as an antidote—a stimulus to spur a person on to calm caution. Fear draws to itself objects of fear, as a magnet draws to itself pieces of iron.

Fear intensifies and magnifies our physical pain and mental agonies a hundredfold. Fear is destructive to the heart, nervous system, and brain. It is destructive to mental initiative, courage, judgment, common sense, and will power. Fear shrouds the soul's all-conquering confidence and power.

When something is threatening to harm you, do not throttle your creative mental powers with fear. Instead, use fear as a goad to find practical solutions to avoid danger.

When something is threatening you, do not sit idle—do

something about it, calmly mustering all the power of your will and judgment.

Fear of failure or sickness is nourished by thinking constantly of dire possibilities, until these take root in the subconscious and finally in the superconscious. These fear seeds germinate and fill the mind with fear plants bearing poisonous, fear fruits.

If you are unable to dislodge the haunting fear of failure or ill health, divert your mind by turning your attention to interesting, absorbing books, or even to harmless amusements. After the mind forgets its haunting fear, encourage it to discover and root out the causes of failure and ill health in the soil of your daily life.

Do not fear disease or accidents if you have had them once. Rather, fear to be afraid, for such fear will create disease- and accident-consciousness, and if it is strong enough, you will draw to yourself the very things you most fear. On the other hand, fearlessness will, in all probability, avert them, or at least minimize their power.

Kill fear by refusing to be afraid. Know that you are safe behind the battlements of God's eternal safety, even though you are rocked on seas of suffering, or find death knocking at your door. God's protecting rays can dispel the menacing clouds of doomsday, calm the waves of trials, and keep you safe, whether you are in a castle or on the battlefield of life, with bullets of trials flying around you.

When fear comes, tense and relax, and exhale several times. Switch on the electricity of calmness and nonchalance. Let your whole mental machinery wake up and actively hum with the vibration of will. Then, harness the power of will to the cogwheels of fearless caution and good judgment. Continuously revolve these to produce practical ideas for escaping your specific, impending calamity.

A mental indulgence in fear will create a subconscious fear habit. Then, when something upsetting to the regular routine occurs, the subconscious fear habit will assert itself, magnify the object of your fears, and paralyze the will-to-fight-fear faculty of the conscious mind.

Since you are made in God's image, you have all the powers and potentialities of God. It is wrong to think that your trials are greater than your divinity. Remember, no matter what your tests are, you are not too weak to fight them. God will not allow you to be tried beyond your strength.

Fear should not produce mental inertia, paralysis, or despondency. Instead, it should spur you on to calm, cautious activity, avoiding equally rashness and timidity.

Uproot fear from within by forceful concentration on courage—and by shifting your consciousness to the absolute peace within. Associate with healthy and prosperous people who do not fear sickness or failure.

⇢8⇠

Worry

No matter how busy you are, do not forget occasionally to free your mind completely from worries and all duties. Dismiss them from your mind. Remember, you were not made for them; they were made by you. Do not allow them to torture you.

When you are beset by overwhelming mental trials or worries, try to fall asleep. If you can do that, you will find on awakening that that worry has loosened its grip upon you. Tell yourself that even if you died, the earth would continue to follow its orbit, and business would be carried on as usual; hence, why worry? When you take yourself too seriously, death comes along to mock you and remind you of the brevity of material life and its duties.

Mental relaxation consists in the ability to free the attention at will from haunting worries over past and present difficulties, dread of accidents, or disturbing thoughts and attachments. Mastery in mental relaxation comes with faithful practice. It can be attained by freeing the mind of all thoughts at will and keeping the attention fixed on peace and contentment within. By faithful practice you can divert the attention from worry to peace through meditation.

Any time you are tired or worried, inhale and tense, then throw your breath out and relax your whole body; remain without thought or breath for a few moments, and you will become calm.

Let go of your worries. Enter into absolute silence every morning and night. Try to remain for one minute at a time without thinking, especially if you are worried. Then try to remain several minutes with a quiet mind. Then visualize some happy incident in your life; mentally go through the pleasant experience over and over again until you forget your worries entirely.

→9←

Worry Fasting

If you are suffering from mental ill health, go on a mental diet. A health-giving mental fast will clear the mind and rid it of the accumulated mental poisons resulting from a careless, faulty mental diet. First of all, learn to remove the cause of your worries without permitting them to worry you. Do not feed your mind with daily created mental poisons of fresh worries.

Worries are often the result of attempting to do too many things hurriedly. Do not "bolt" your mental duties, but thoroughly masticate them, one at a time, with the teeth of attention, and saturate them with the saliva of good judgment. Thus you will avoid worry indigestion.

Whenever you make up your mind not to worry and decide to go on a worry fast, stick to your resolution. You can stop worrying entirely. Say to yourself: "I can do only my best; no more. I am satisfied and happy that I am doing my best to solve my problem; there is absolutely no reason why I should worry."

When you are on a worry fast, drink copiously of the fresh waters of peace flowing from the spring of every circumstance, vitalized by your determination to be cheerful. If you have made up your mind to be cheerful, nothing can make you unhappy. If you do not choose to destroy your peace of mind by accepting the suggestion of unhappy circumstances, no one can make you dejected. Be concerned only with the untiring performance of right actions and not with their results. Leave the latter to God, saying, "I have done my best under the circumstances. Therefore, I am happy."

Three times a day, shake off all worries. At seven o'clock in the morning, say to yourself: "All my worries of the night are cast out, and from 7 to 8 a.m. I refuse to worry, no matter how troublesome are the duties ahead of me. I am on a worry fast."

From noon to 1 p.m. say, "I am cheerful, I will not worry."

In the evening, between six and nine o'clock, while in the company of your husband or wife or "hard-to-get-along-with" relatives or friends, mentally make a strong resolution: "Within these three hours I will not worry; I refuse to get vexed, even if I am nagged. No matter how tempting it is to indulge in a worry feast, I will resist the temptation. I must not paralyze my peace-heart by shocks of worries. I cannot afford to worry."

After you succeed in carrying out worry fasts during certain hours of the day, try doing it for one or two weeks at a time, and then try to prevent the accumulation of worry poisons in your system entirely. Whenever you find yourself indulging in a worry feast, go on a partial or complete worry fast for a day or a week.

Although the negative method for overcoming worry poisoning is worry fasting, there are also positive methods. A person infected with the germs of worry must feast regularly on the society of joyful minds. Every day he must associate, if only for a little while, with "joy-infected" minds.

There are some people the song of whose laughter nothing can still. Seek them out and feast with them on this most vitalizing food of joy. Continue the laughter diet for a month or two, feasting on laughter in the company of really joyful people. Digest it thoroughly by whole-heartedly masticating laughter with the teeth of your attention. Steadfastly continue your laughter diet once you have begun it, and at the end of a month or two you will see the change—your mind will be filled with sunshine. Remember, specific habits can be changed only by specific habit-forming actions.

10

Nervousness

Fear, worry, and anger are the mental causes of nervousness. When you are angry, you poison the blood and burn the nerves. Anger changes the chemicals in the blood and affects circulation. When wrath comes, you become the tool of ignorance and do wrong things. When you worry, you paralyze the nerves.

The cure is to be calm at all times and to do your best. If something has gone wrong, correct the error. Look at things intelligently and peacefully, and you will gain the right understanding.

Cultivate peace, calmness, and cheerfulness. The more cheerful and calm you are, the better it is for you. The more you worry, or are angry or afraid, the less poise you have. The more peace you have, the less nervousness.

You will find that there is a law of God that will protect you. Your nervousness will disappear when you realize that you are one with God. You must realize that you are not this flesh but the Spirit behind the flesh.

Every night before going to bed, say: "I am a Prince of Peace sitting on the throne of Poise."

11

Materialism

Do material things bring joy? No, they bring a little pleasure for a while, but sorrow always follows. They promise joy, but they do not keep their promise. Those who amuse themselves in life too much with material, earthly pleasures will lose their happiness; those who over-indulge in sex lose their vitality; those who eat too much lose their health and the satisfaction in eating. Everywhere you go people are reaping the harvest of wild oats sown earlier in life.

Too much concern for physical luxuries and unnecessary "necessities" makes people forget the need for developing mental efficiency in everything, and for acquiring divine contentment. Because of the time-consuming demands of Tyrant Physical Luxury, there is no time to develop mental efficiency or to cultivate peace.

Every man must remember that the real needs of life are mental and spiritual efficiency. The Goal: Maximum peace, all-round mental efficiency, and sufficient material security.

12

If you covered a gold image with a black cloth, would you then say that the image had become black? Of course not! You would know that, behind the veil, the image was still gold.

So will it be when you tear away the black veil of ignorance which now hides your soul. You will behold again the unchanging beauty of your own divine nature.

Chapter 5

Cultivate Good Habits

→1←

If a bad habit bothers you, do two things. Try to avoid it and everything that stimulates it, without concentrating on it in your zeal to avoid it. Then divert your mind to some good habit, and keep the mind furiously engaged in cultivating the good habit, until it becomes a part of yourself.

→2←

A good habit is your greatest friend—a bad habit, your mortal enemy. Be careful about the repetition of an action. It will become a habit before you realize it. Habit is second nature, but it can be changed by persistent good action.

→3←

Wherever you are, remain awake and alive with your thought, perception, and intuition—ever ready, like a good photographer, to take pictures of exemplary conduct and to ignore bad behavior. Your highest happiness lies in your being ever ready to learn, and to behave properly. The more you improve yourself, the more you will elevate others around you. The self-improving man is an increasingly happy man.

→4←

Be careful in your choice of company. Keep company with people who are calm, strong, and wise, with a deeper nature than you have. When a criminal is put in the company of a greater criminal, that does not help him. When it is time for him to leave prison, the warden says, "When are you coming back?" When nervous people are in the company of other nervous people, they cannot get better. Always choose calm company.

→5←

Don't let unhealthy materials float down the stream of your habit-forming thoughts. Watch the quality of the books you read. Watch the influence on you of family and close friends who constantly associate with you. Many people are unsuccessful because their families have infected their subconscious minds with progress-paralyzing, discouraging thoughts.

6

Some people require much time to form mental habits of health, prosperity, and the acquisition of wisdom. Actually, the time needed for this purpose can be shortened. Slow or rapid habit formation depends on the general state of health, on the condition of the brain cells and nervous system, and on the type of habit-forming methods used. Most people are halfhearted in their thoughts and actions—hence, they do not succeed. A mental habit, in order to materialize, must be strong and persistent.

For instance, the prosperity or health habit must be cultivated by thoughts of prosperity or health until results are apparent. An unfailingly wholesome, courageous mental attitude is absolutely necessary to the attainment of one's needs and wants.

While an inattentive, scatterbrained person requires a long time to form even a simple habit, an intelligent, purposeful individual can easily form a good mental habit in a trice, by the mere wish. Therefore, if you have a mental, physical, or spiritual habit that impedes your progress, rid yourself of it now. Do not put it off.

7

Perform every action, insignificant or important, with quick, alert attention. Remember, attention is the needle that cuts grooves in the record of your memory cells. A man without attention lacks the instrument that awakens memory. Absentmindedness blunts the needle of attention.

Deep, alert attention with feeling is the needle that cuts grooves in the record of your memory cells.

8

Perform little duties very well. Do you know that you have been using only 5 or 6 percent of your attention in your vocation? Henceforth, you ought to apply 100 percent concentration while doing your work.

All good work is God's work, if you perform it with divine consciousness. The only materialistic work is that which is done with a purely selfish motive. In earning money, always think you are doing so for your fellow beings, even if you have no family. Destroy the false division between material and spiritual work.

⇾9⇽

Memory should be trained and used to recall only noble and uplifting experiences. Only the good that is gleaned from an experience should be allowed into the reservoir of memory. If any slimy thoughts find their way into this reservoir, those same thoughts will emerge as words or actions at some unexpected time. If only good is present, then only good can come forth. Guard well the gate of your mind.

⇾10⇽

It is not your passing thoughts or brilliant ideas but your everyday habits that control your life. Habits of thought are mental magnets; they draw to themselves specific objects relative to the quality of their magnetism.

⇾11⇽

When the soul's natural happiness becomes encrusted with the temporary pleasures of the senses, then the golden luster of the soul becomes obscured.

Many think they cannot live without evil, misery-producing pleasures, such as, for example, the taking of body-killing alcohol. But these very people, if they were to form good habits, would say: "We cannot live without the peace and pleasure of meditation. We are miserable when we indulge in lesser pleasures."

Just as a person must part with little sums of money to invest for future greater gain, so the devotee must forego the indulgence in material pleasures for the sake of gaining the pure joy of meditation. Thousands fail to understand why the pleasure-producing senses overshadow the joy of Spirit.

The purpose of self-control is a spiritual business proposition designed to bring the greatest happiness to man. Man is made in the image of God, and as such has within himself the latent, everlasting joy of Spirit, as a tree is hidden in the seed. Just as roasted seeds do not germinate, so, when the joy-seed of the soul is scorched by the flames of material desires, it fails to produce the immortal tree of happiness.

Cultivate the habit of contacting superior soul joy immediately upon awakening. Then, while filled with the joy of the soul, one may enjoy such harmless pleasures as eating, meeting friends, and so forth, without attachment. In this way the soul can spiritualize all material enjoyments.

12

Almost every soul is a prisoner of the senses, which are entrenched on the surface of the body. The soul's attention is lured away from its inner kingdom in the medulla, the spiritual eye, and the chakras to the outer regions of the body, where greed, temptation, and attachment have their strongholds. The devotee who wants to lead King Soul away from the misery-making slums of the senses finds that he cannot do so without a severe clash between the soldiers of the senses and the divine soldiers of the soul.

When the devotee passes through the initial state of meditation and arrives at the middle state of Self-realization, he realizes that his good and bad habits have gathered together on the battlefield of consciousness, pitted against one another.

Meditation is the inner war-drum that rouses good and bad habits from the slumber of indifference and makes them want to increase their forces in order to attain victory over the consciousness of the devotee. When one is totally under the influence of bad habits, he does not find any resistance from the good habits. It is only when the devotee tries to cultivate good habits of concentration, calmness, and peace that the bad habits of fickleness, restlessness, and disquietude create psychological resistance.

The enthusiastic spiritual beginner, in his zeal as he first tries to meditate, does not realize the resistance of bad habits. The bad habits do not notice the silent invasion of good habits in the spiritual beginner. Only when the spiritual seeker means business and struggles repeatedly to establish good habits in the kingdom of consciousness do the bad habits become afraid and make furious attempts to oust the good intruders.

When the seeker begins to use soul perception and good habits to fight the bad habits, he realizes that his heart is filled with compassion for the bad habits, for they seem to be his own, and dear to him. In other words, the devotee, in spite of knowing what he should do, discovers it is hard to dislodge the dear old habits of restlessness, constant action, wrong eating, and sense pleasures by the pitiless fiery soldiers of calmness, ecstasy, and self-control.

13

The grand method of killing bad habits lies in the actual performance of God-awakening, good habits of meditation.

When the habit of delusion precedes the habit of wisdom and settles in the soul, the only way out is to use will power to meditate deeply and daily until the all-alluring, bliss-contact of God is definitely achieved and can be reproduced in the consciousness at will.

→14←

It is just as easy to be peaceful and joyful as to be worried and disturbed. Never forget to smile—not a mask-like smile without sincerity behind it, but the honest, radiant smile that comes from a light, joyful heart.

Develop the habit of smiling, no matter what happens, and get complete control of your thoughts. They absolutely make or mar your life.

People pay entirely too much attention to their physical being and think too much about what they should eat and how much they should rest. It is all a matter of will. I have never been tired in my life, and I get along on as little as five hours' sleep a month. I never eat in the morning, and for lunch I have a light meal—preferably uncooked fruits and chopped nuts, with an occasional egg. For supper I take only a salad. But my whole life has been given over to the study of Yogoda.* What I have done, others can do also.

15

Good habits are your best helpers; preserve their force by stimulating them with good actions. Bad habits are your worst enemies; against your will, they make you do things that hurt you. Starve bad habits by refusing to give them any further food of bad actions.

True freedom consists in doing things in accordance with right judgment, and not from the compulsion of habits. Eat what you should eat and not necessarily what you are used to eating. Do what you ought, not what your habits dictate.

Good and bad habits take some time to acquire force. Powerful bad habits can be displaced by opposite good habits if the latter are patiently cultured. First crowd out all bad habits by good habits in everything, then cultivate the consciousness of being free from *all* habits.

* PUBLISHER'S NOTE: Yogoda is a name Yogananda created in the early years for describing his teachings. He translated it poetically as "harmonious development of all human faculties." Translated literally, it means "that which imparts yoga, or divine union."

The Parable of the Wheat and the Tares [Weeds]

Another parable put he forth unto them, saying, The kingdom of heaven is likened unto a man which sowed good seed in his field: But while men slept, his enemy came and sowed tares [weeds] among the wheat, and went his way. But when the blade was sprung up, and brought forth fruit, then appeared the tares also. So the servants of the householder came and said unto him, Sir, didst not thou sow good seed in thy field? from whence then hath it tares? He said unto them, An enemy hath done this. The servants said unto him, Wilt thou then that we go and gather them up? But he said, Nay, lest while ye gather up the tares, ye root up also the wheat with them. Let both grow together until the harvest: and in the time of harvest I will say to the reapers, Gather ye together first the tares, and bind them in bundles to burn them: but gather the wheat into my barn. (MATT. 13:24–30)

Interpretation

The kingdom of God-realization can be compared to a man who, by deep, daily meditation, sowed good seeds of spiritual experiences in the field of his consciousness, but while he slept (was unaware of spiritual perceptions), his enemy of subconscious tendencies grew weeds of material habits among the wheat of spiritual Self-realization. When the blades of spiritual development grew and brought forth fruits of spiritual bliss and wisdom, he found he was also hounded by weeds of inner doubts, fears, and a sense of hopelessness about solving the mysteries of God.

The servants (self-control and spiritual discipline) asked their master, "O devotee, whence did these weeds of spiritual obstacles arise in you?" The devotee answered, "Subconscious bad tendencies have secretly grown weeds of material habits along with my spiritual habits."

The servants asked, "Do you want your servants of self-control to go into the subconscious mind and remove the deep-rooted weeds?"

The devotee answered: "Do not waste your time concentrating on negative, unspiritual habits, for in doing so you might lose some spiritual habits because of not being able to focus on their growth. Go on cultivating the good spiritual habits, and don't worry about the unspiritual habits, until the harvest of divine ecstasy and joy-contact with God arrives. In the time of divine ecstasy, the expert reapers of spiritual perception and spiritual habits can gather the weeds of all past incarnations from the subconscious mind, and burn them up with the instantaneously annihilating power of wisdom and the light accumulated in the brain through the interiorized mind."

In meditation and sleep, the mind and energy retire into the spine and brain and obliterate habits of worries and disquietude. In sleep, the energy dispels worries only temporarily. In deep meditation, the superconscious uses the relaxed energy of the mind, concentrated in the brain, to go deep into the brain grooves where habits are secreted, and cauterize evil habits.

Chapter 6

Use the Power of Your Mind

⇾1⇽
A Great Failure Who Became a Great Success

As there are naturally successful people, so there are also habitual failures. John, my friend and student, was such a born failure. He was young, intelligent, and diligent, but it seemed that no matter what job or business he tried, he failed. Harassed, deserted, and penniless, he sought my advice.

He said: "Sir, I am a great failure. For some mysterious reason, not only do I lose my job, but also, after employing me, my employer loses his business. I hate to seek a job for fear of destroying the business of my new employer through the deathly grip of my failure vibration. I am labeled a failure by all of my friends, and I thoroughly believe that I can never succeed."

Through my influence, John got a job in a small business concern. I advised him to affirm daily, before going to bed and upon waking, "Day by day, in every way, I am succeeding more and more in my job."

A month passed and John warned me: "Honored Sir, the business concern you got me into is getting into worse and worse trouble. Please remove me before it goes onto the rocks completely. Perhaps my resignation will save the business from destruction."

I laughed and told John to keep up his affirmation of success and to hold on to his job. After a fortnight John came to me one evening and, with a sigh of relief, exclaimed, "It happened." I asked, "What happened?" "Well, my employer's business collapsed, as I told you it would."

I turned to John and remonstrated: "Every night and every morning, while you have been mentally parroting the affirmation, 'Day by day I am getting better and better,' in the background of your mind, a little octopus of obstinacy has kept on repeating, 'You simpleton, you know that day by day, in every way, you are getting worse and worse.'" He admitted the truth of this.

Smilingly, I reminded John to cast out all negative vibrations during a positive affirmation, because a convinced, conscious mind influences the subconscious, which in turn influences the conscious mind through the power of habit.

I told John that his success was conditioned by his creative ability, his environment, and his prenatal and postnatal habits, and that if he contacted the all-powerful superconscious mind, then alone could he create the cause for absolute success.

I succeeded in getting John a job in another and bigger business. After six months (the longest period he'd ever held a job), he said to me, "Sir, get me out quick. Business is getting pretty bad."

I paid no attention to John's misgivings and told him to go on with his job. After a few weeks, John smilingly moaned, "Sir, the second business you got me into has evaporated too." I pretended to feel sorrowful at his plight, and calmly said, "Never mind, John, I will get you another job."

"Well, Sir," he said, "If you can bear the sin of causing other peoples' businesses to collapse through contact with me, then find me another job."

By continuous effort and influence, I at last secured for John a good job in a very big concern. A year passed and nothing happened, although almost every week John wanted to give up his job, fearing that he would cause the collapse of this third business.

Finally, I asked John to invest his money in a business of his own. He was beside himself with fear, and shouted at me, "If I invest the money I have saved, I am sure to lose it." I firmly assured him: "Of course you must invest your money and energy in some good project, like order-supplying of stationery, which requires no large investment or overhead. I am sure you will succeed."

In the course of a few years, John found himself owning a few successful chain stores and a large amount of capital.

When John was thoroughly convinced of his success, he found himself succeeding in everything he undertook. One day he laughingly said: "Through God and through your help, I am changed from a great failure to a great success. Please tell me how this happened. I can understand my own failure owing to lack of understanding, but I cannot understand how I demolished other peoples' businesses by the power of my failure vibration."

I replied: "You did not destroy the businesses you were in. The law of attraction that governs people of like vibrations was at work. You attracted a business about to fail, and vice versa, like two lighted bombs rolling down the hill side by side. You were a failure and the business was about to fail. By the law of inner affinity, you went down the hill of failure together and exploded at the same time."

The Western brothers must learn that the mind is greater than its inventions. More time should be given to the art of controlling the mind for scientifically achieving all-round success. Less time should be spent pursuing the products of mind at the cost of neglecting the cultivation of the all-accomplishing, all-powerful mind itself. Follow the way taught by India of acquiring superconsciousness and absolute control over the mind, and thus learn to create at will what you need.

→2←

Mind is the source of all your troubles and all your happiness. You are stronger than all your tests. If you don't realize it now, you will have to realize it later. God has given you the power to control your mind and body and thus be free from pain and sorrow. Never say, "I am through." Do not poison your mind by thinking that if you cannot get certain foods you will suffer, and so on.

Never allow your mind to entertain thoughts of illness or limitation, and you will see your body change for the better. Mind is the power that is creating this body, and if the mind is weak, the body becomes weak. Don't grieve or worry about anything.

If you strengthen your mind, you will not feel bodily pains. No matter what happens, you must be absolutely free in your mind.

→3←

Use constructively the power you already have, and more will come. Tune yourself with Cosmic Power. Then you will possess the creative power of Spirit. You will be in contact with Infinite Intelligence, which can guide you and solve all problems. Power from the dynamic Source of your being will flow through you so that you will be creative in the world of business, the world of thought, or the world of wisdom.

→4←

God gave you will power, concentration, faith, reason, and common sense to help yourself. You must use them all as you seek the divine help, but you must not rely wholly on your ego and thus disconnect yourself from the divine force.

During affirmations or prayer, always feel that you are using *your own, but God-given* power to heal yourself or others. Always believe that as God's beloved child, you are using the will and reason He has given you. A balance must be struck between the old idea of wholly depending on God, and the modern way of sole dependence on the ego.

5

Every word you utter must represent not only Truth, but some of your realized soul force. Words that are saturated with sincerity, conviction, faith, and intuition are like highly explosive vibration bombs, which can explode the rocks of difficulties and create the change desired. Avoid speaking unpleasant words, even if they are true.

Sincere words or affirmations* repeated understandingly, feelingly, and willingly are sure to move the omnipresent Cosmic Vibratory Force and render you aid in your difficulty. Appeal to that Force with infinite confidence, casting out all doubt. Do not keep looking for the desired result—you cannot sow the vibratory prayer seed in the soil of cosmic consciousness and then dig it up every minute to see if it has germinated.

6

In all affirmations the intensity of attention comes first, but continuity and repetition also count a great deal. Impreg-

* Publisher's Note: For more information on affirmations and how to use them, see *How to Have Courage, Calmness, and Confidence* by Paramhansa Yogananda, and *Affirmations for Self-Healing* by Swami Kriyananda, Crystal Clarity Publishers, Nevada City, California.

nate your affirmations with your devotion, will, and faith, repeating them intensely, unmindful of the results that will come naturally as the fruit of your labors.

As you try to heal yourself, your attention must not be on the disease, which always damps the faith, but on the mind. During mental cures of fear, anger, or any bad habit, the concentration should be on the opposite positive quality. For example, the cure for fear is culturing the consciousness of courage; of anger—peace; of weakness—strength; of sickness—health.

In trying to get rid of a physical or mental sickness, one often concentrates more on the gripping power of the disease than on the possibility of cure, and thus permits the disease to become a mental as well as a physical habit.

Chronic mental or physical diseases always have a deep root in the subconscious mind. That is why all affirmations practiced by the conscious mind should be impressive enough to transform the subconscious mind, which will in turn automatically influence the conscious mind.

Still stronger conscious will or devotion affirmations reach not only the subconscious but also the superconscious mind, the magic storehouse of all miraculous mental powers.

Individual affirmations should be practiced willingly, feelingly, intelligently, and devotionally, once in a while loudly, but mostly mentally (not even in a whisper), with ever-increasing intensity of attention and continuity. The attention from the very beginning of affirmation must steadily increase and should never be allowed to flag. Flagging attention, like a truant child, should be brought back again and again, and patiently trained to perform its given task.

Attentive, intelligent repetition and patience are the creators of habits and should be employed during all affirmations. Such deep and long-continued affirmations should be practiced mentally until they become a part of one's intuitional convictions. It is better to die (if death has to come) with the conviction of being cured than with the consciousness of a mental or bodily ailment being incurable.

All affirmations, in order to reach the superconscious, must be free from uncertainty, doubt, and inattention. Attention and devotion are lights that can lead even blindly uttered affirmations to the subconscious and superconscious minds.

Apply these instructions as you repeat this affirmation:

Yogananda's Affirmation for Psychological Success

I am brave, I am strong.
Perfume of success thought
Blows in me, blows in me.
I am cool, I am calm,
I am sweet, I am kind,
I am love, I am sympathy,
I am charming and magnetic,
I am pleased with all.
I wipe away all tears and fears,
I have no enemy,
I am the friend of all.
I have no habits,
In eating, dressing, behaving;
I am free, I am free.
I command Thee, O Attention,
To come and practice concentration

On things I do, on works I do.
I can do everything
When so I think, when so I think.
In church or temple, in prayer mood,
My vagrant thoughts against me stood
And held my mind from reaching Thee,
And held my mind from reaching Thee.
Teach me to own again, oh, own again,
My matter-sold mind and brain,
That I may give them to Thee
In prayer and ecstasy
In meditation and reverie.
I shall worship Thee
In meditation and seclusion.
I shall feel Thine energy
Flowing through my hands in activity.
Lest I lose Thee,
I shall find Thee in activity.

→7←

Your success in life depends not only upon natural ability; it also depends upon your determination to grasp the opportunities presented to you. Opportunities in life come by creation, not by chance. They are created by *you*, either now or at some time in the recent or distant past. Since you have earned them, use them to the best advantage.

You can make your life much more worthwhile, now and in the future, if you focus your attention on your immediate needs, and use all your abilities and available information to fulfill them. You must develop *all* the powers that God gave you, the unlimited powers that come from the innermost forces of your being.

→8←

Your thoughts will inevitably bring you either to failure or to success—*according to which thought is the strongest.* Therefore, you must thoroughly believe in your own plans, use your talents to carry them out, and be receptive so that God can work through you. His laws work at all times. You are always demonstrating success or failure, according to the kind of thoughts you *habitually* entertain. If your trend of thought is ordinarily negative, an occasional positive thought is not enough to change the vibration to one of success.

9

Hope is the eternal light on the dark pathway through which the soul must travel for incarnations in order to reach God.

Human beings hope and try for a while, but if they fail a dozen times, they cease to hope and become despondent. The divine man never ceases to hope, for he knows that he has all eternity in which to materialize his dreams.

To kill hope and be despondent is to put on an animal mask of limitation and to hide your divine identity of almightiness. Instead, hope for the highest and the best, for, as a child of God, nothing is too good for you. Keep on hoping. Hope is born from the intuitive knowing of the soul that eventually we will remember the forgotten image of God within us.

10

The man of powerful concentration must ask God to direct his focused mind on the right path for success. Passive people want God to do all the work, and egotists ascribe all their success to themselves. Passive people do not use the power of God as intelligence. Egotists, though using God-given intelligence, forget to ask God's guidance as to how the intelligence should be used. It hurts me to see egotists fail after making true, intelligent effort.

It is necessary to avoid both passivity and egotism. In the early morning and before going to bed, every man, woman, and child must make contact with God in order to succeed.

Your soul's message cannot reach God through your mental microphone if it is broken by the hammers of restlessness. You must repair that microphone by practicing deep silence both in the morning and before sleep, until all restless thoughts disappear. Then, affirm deeply, "My Father and I are One," until you feel the response of God as deep, increasing peace. This peace will not be felt except through practice of the right method of meditation. This increasing peace, or bliss, is the surest proof of God's contact and response.

You must broadcast your message, "My Father and I are One," until you feel the overpowering, all-solacing bliss of God. When this happens, you have made contact. Then demand your celestial right by affirming, "Father, I am Thy child. Guide me to my right prosperity," or, "Father, I will reason, I will will, I will act, but guide Thou my reason, will, and activity to the right thing I should do in order to acquire health, wealth, peace, and wisdom."

Do not will and act first, but contact God first and thus harness your will and activity to the right goal.

As you cannot receive an answer by calling someone through a microphone and then running away, so, also, you must not pray once and run away, but continuously broadcast your prayer to God through your calm mental microphone *until* you hear His voice. Most people pray with restlessness; they do not pray determined to receive a response.

Remember that the surest way to all-round prosperity—or to the attainment of health, wealth, peace, and wisdom—lies in first reclaiming your lost divine birthright by continuously broadcasting your message to God through your calm mental microphone *until* you receive His answer through the increased bliss of meditation.

Chapter 7

Discover Your True Nature in Silence

⇾1⇽

Because of long concentration upon the little body and its necessities, the soul has forgotten its omnipresent nature. God is omnipresent. Man's soul, made in His image, has in it the seed experience of omnipresence. That omnipresence is hidden in the little soul as a tree is secreted in a small seed.

Looking at the body daily causes the mind to think of itself as confined in flesh. The mind, meditating upon the body, becomes limited by it. The mind, meditating upon the Infinite, becomes unlimited. Meditation upon the Infinite, as it grows deeper, convinces the mind that it is not encased only in the little body, but is in everything.

The spiritual man, through the spreading light of sympathy and meditation, learns to feel the woes and pains of other souls. He feels that the world is his home. That is why the meditating aspirant must do away with little body attachments. He must learn to be proof against warm or cold climates. He must learn to overcome hunger and pain. He must learn to conquer all the attachments that govern the little body, for as long as the mind is focused on the body, the soul cannot remember its omnipresent nature.

Meditation means constant thinking of the vastness within and without, so that the soul may forget its attachment to the little body and may remember its vast body as God.

→2←

You have wandered in the wilderness of distraction, far from your home of peace. You are a prodigal son who wants to go back to your home of happiness. The Father is waiting. Do not be a beggar imprisoned within the self-erected walls of limitations. Break the walls. Try to be a good son instead of a truant one.

Meditate, and then broadcast your prayer-demands through your calm mind-microphone. Loudly, softly, and mentally affirm, "Father, Thou and I are One," until you feel Oneness, not only in conscious intelligence or subconscious imagination, but in your superconscious conviction.

When your message of yearning reaches God in this way, you will feel His response. Keep your mind-radio finely tuned with soft touches of deepest devotion and the grandest, most constant love.

Then, suddenly, He may burst upon you clearly as a song, a cosmic voice, or the fragrance of a trillion mystic flowers. The surest sign of His presence is the dawn of peace, which is the first messenger to herald His secret approach. Then peace bursts into more dazzling lights of endless joy, and you behold Him in the light of increasing, ever-charming, ever-new joy.

You can never attract this messenger until you open the secret door of deepest meditation. When the contact is made through increasing peace and joy, tell your Father that you are no longer a prodigal son. Tell Him again and again, deeply, with your superconscious conviction, that you and He are one. You are back to stay in His mansion.

When your Father accepts your supreme demand of oneness with Him, then demand the lesser things: prosperity, power, wisdom, or anything you like. You will then receive your divine birthright.

→3←

If one is nervous and keeps his body in constant motion, his Life Force is restless, his mind is restless, his vitality is restless, and his breath is restless. But if one controls the Life Force by spiritual exercises and the practice of calmness through meditation, then his mind and vital power are within his control.

Attaining calm breath by proper breathing exercises, one can achieve great concentration. By mental concentration and self-control, as in meditation, one finds the breath and the Life Force automatically calmed; thus, stability of character is attained.

→4←

Practice the art of silence. The tigers of worries, sickness, and death are running after you, and the only place you can be safe is in silence.

The more you are silent, the more you will find happiness. Those who meditate deeply feel a wonderful silence, which should be maintained when in the company of people. What you learn in meditation, practice in activity and conversation, and let no one dislodge your calmness. Hold on to your peace.

When you meet people, do not become affected by their state of consciousness. When they are singing of God, be one with them, but if they show undesirable qualities, stand aloof. Meet people with silence, eat with silence, and work with silence. God loves silence.

→5←

The moon's reflection in a pot of swirling water looks ruffled, but the moon is never distorted—it is the disturbed water that produces the illusion. Calm the water in the pot, and you will find the perfect, undistorted image of the moon.

The perfect image of God within you is distorted by your mental restlessness and lack of conviction. Your celestial abilities lie within you unharmed; it is the waves of your environment-grown, wrong convictions and subconscious bad habits that make the powerful image within you look distorted. Learn to calm your mental waves by the magic wand of super-concentration, and you will behold, undistorted, your perfect all-conquering ability.

→6←

God came with you in the beginning and has been with you all the time. He alone will be with you when you go. Make peace with Him now. No duty is more important than your duty to God, for no duty is performed without God's power.

7

Man is operating five telephones—the senses of sight, sound, smell, taste, and touch—controlled by the medulla and the heart. The heart and the medulla are the switchboards through which these telephones contact the brain. When a sensation reaches the brain, that sensation immediately rouses thoughts. The scientific way to do away with thought is to withdraw the attention from objects of the senses.

Through meditation you learn how to disconnect your energy from the senses* and consciously go into the Infinite. You experience an expansion of consciousness from the boundaries of the body to the boundaries of eternity.

Unless you absolutely free the temple of attention from disturbing thoughts, God will not come. God doesn't surrender Himself unless He is sure that every worldly thought is removed from your mind. He is like a candle flame that cannot stand the gusts of restlessness. He will burn steadily when you are free from restlessness.

* Publisher's Note: The *Hong-Sau* Technique in chapter 9 is especially effective for disconnecting energy from the senses.

→8←

We teach a scientific method of concentration. A popular, ineffectual method of concentration may be depicted by this useless attempt:

The scene is an apartment, about 2 P.M. on a wintry day. A lady enters, pulls down the shades, and hurries to sit in a straight-backed chair to concentrate. No sooner has her body touched the chair than she exclaims: "My goodness, this seat is too hard. Let me fetch a pillow." Seated on the pillow, she suddenly discovers that the chair is maliciously squeaking and disturbing the beginnings of her concentration. So she transfers her pillow and her body to another chair.

"Now, at last, everything is right for a delightful dip into the depths of concentration." Only a moment passes and she is about to plunge within, when, "*Ta, ta, ta, ta, tang, ta, ta, tang*" sings out the boiling radiator. In disgust, she chokes the radiator's voice. In righteous indignation she now increases her determination to dive deep into the heart of meditation.

A moment later, "*Plung, ploong, ploong-plung*" goes the piano in the apartment next door. Annoyed, she thinks, "There goes that terrible piano again, just as I sit down to meditate."

As her wrath calms down in the semi-darkness, she begins to think, "Well, that's really a fairly good piano; it only needs a little tuning." Then comes the memory of her dear grandmother's piano in the sweet old days of long ago—her dear grandmother, who always protected her from the harsh discipline of her parents . . . and more loving thoughts of her grandmother.

Suddenly, she jerks herself from her sweet reverie and remembers, "Oh, I must practice silence; I must concentrate." So, with saintly dignity, her spirit rebuked for its restlessness, with rather battered self-control, she once more attempts to meditate.

Her eyes have hardly closed again when "*Gr Gr Grr Grrrrrr*— " crows out the telephone with impudent, patience-piercing pertinacity. She breathes to herself through grinding teeth, "I will not answer. Crow all you like, Mr. Telephone." But "*Grrrrrr*" goes the impertinent bell with unimaginable persistency.

"Well, maybe it is an important call. 'Hello, there—What is it you want? This is Somerville 2924. . . .'" As she hears the soul-exasperating answer, "Wrong number," she slams the mouthpiece onto the hook.

This terrible ordeal over, she musters enough courage to again try to concentrate, while her brain is seething with the thought: "I will break that telephone forever and ever. It will then disturb me no more." With scissors in hand, she is about to cut the cord when she thinks of the inconvenience that might follow, so she changes her mind and puts a piece of cardboard between the hammer and the bell on the telephone.

That accomplished, victorious, she sits once more on her throne of concentration. A few more minutes pass and she is half-dozing, due to her successive battles with piano noises, the telephone, and so forth. Catching herself sleeping, half-ashamed, she sits up straight once more to begin again to meditate. Immediately there arises a clamorous ringing of her doorbell. As before, she thinks, "I will not answer it."

The doorbell goes on ringing until she thinks again, "Maybe it is something important." At the door she assumes a galvanized smile as she greets her three lady friends, who have all obtained a master's degree in the art of gossiping, and she gushes, "How do you do? Come right in, you three darlings. I'm so delighted that you've come over." Behind the forced smile lies the silent whispering, "Oh, you pests and gossips, when will you go so that I can concentrate?"

Three hours slip away as she merrily laughs at the folly of her three gossiping cronies. At last, the door closes behind their vanishing forms. Much relieved, the lady once more sits down to seek her lost throne of silence, but her attention is mobbed by memories of radiators, piano noises, telephone bells, door bells, and gossips. She looks at her watch and, with a resigned sigh, says, "I give up, dear Concentration. It seems that I cannot be with you today. I have to run now to prepare the evening meal."

The above experience is only a sample of what happens to most women and men whenever they attempt to concentrate.

God tries to speak to His children through the voice of silence and peace in response to His children's prayers, but His voice is usually drowned out by the ringing of telephones, sensations of touch, smell, taste, hearing, and sight, and by the rowdy noises of the sensation- and memory-roused thoughts. Sadly, God turns away.

With blessings
Paramhansa Yogananda
Encinitas - April 3rd 1951
by the sea.

CHAPTER *8*

CONTACT GOD THROUGH DEVOTION, PRAYER, AND MEDITATION

→1←

Resurrect your soul from the dream of frailties. Resurrect your soul in eternal wisdom. What is the method? Relaxation, self-control, right diet, right fortitude, and an undaunted attitude of the mind. Do not acknowledge defeat. To acknowledge defeat brings greater defeat.

You have unlimited power; you must cultivate that power. Meditation is the way to resurrect your soul from the bondage of the body and all your trials. Meditate at the feet of the Infinite. Learn to saturate yourself with God. Your trials may be great, but your greatest enemy is yourself. You are immortal; your trials are mortal. They are changeable, but you are unchangeable. You can unleash the eternal powers and shatter your trials.

→2←

Never mind if you cannot at first contact God or hear His knock at the gate of your heart. For a long time you have been running away from Him, hiding in the marsh of the senses. The noise of your own rowdy passions and the flight of your heavy footsteps in the material world have made you unable to hear His call within. Stop, be calm, meditate deeply, and out of the silence will loom forth the Divine Presence.

God responds to law. All those who conform to the law can test and experience it for themselves. Physical laws have to be interpreted by the physical senses. Divine laws have to be comprehended by concentration, meditation, and intuition. God can never hide from the person who exercises devotion, love, right meditation, and a soul-call. God never fails to listen to soul-calls, but He does not always respond in the way we expect.

When ever-new, ever-increasing joy fills your silence, know that you have contacted God, and that He is answering through your soul.

Use your deepest meditation, mingled with your utmost devotion, in the silent hours of the night, at the break of dawn, or in the hidden glow of twilight, in seeking an answer to your desire. Meditate and use your will power steadily day after day, week after week, year after year, until the cosmic silence of ages is broken and you receive your answer. You will not have to wait for ages, for you will find in deep meditation that God's bliss will surround you and speak to you through the voice of peace.

→3←

You must find out what kind of prayer brings a response from God. Purely intellectual prayers give intellectual satisfaction, but they do not bring a conscious response from God. Emotional prayers give rise to excitement, but devotional prayers bring the calm joy of the soul.

To bring a response to your prayers, you must pray intelligently with a bursting soul, seldom aloud, mostly mentally, without displaying to anyone what is happening within. You must pray with utmost devotion, feeling that God is listening to everything you mentally affirm. Pray into the depths of the night in the seclusion of your soul. Pray until God replies to you through the intelligible voice of bursting joy tingling through every body cell and every thought, or through visions depicting what you should do in a given case.

The increasing joy after meditation is the proof that God has answered through the devotion-tuned radio of your heart. The longer and more deeply you meditate and affirm, the more you will be conscious of the ever-increasing joy in your heart. Then you will know without doubt that there is a God, and that He is ever-existing, ever-conscious, omnipresent, ever-new Joy. Then demand: "Father, now, today, all day, all tomorrows, every instant, in sleep, in wakefulness, all through life, in death, in the beyond, remain with me as the consciously responding joy of my heart.

→4←

The usual method of prayer is, for the most part, ineffective because we do not really mean business with God. He knows what selfish desires we have in our innermost mind; therefore He does not manifest Himself. While the demons of sensations and thoughts dance in the temples of body and mind, it is difficult to recognize God, who remains hidden behind the veil of silence within.

→5←

Most people are absentminded while they pray. Some love God but do not express that love continuously. These prayers are not answered.

Most people beg from God; hence they receive a beggar's pittance instead of a son's share. A beggar supplicates; a child demands. A beggar's plea is of a fawning, groveling, cringing nature; a child's demand is straightforward, sincere, and lovingly unafraid. Those who demand as children receive everything the Father has.

A beggar doubts that his plea will be granted; a true son knows that his demand will be fulfilled. You were a son, but your own weakness has made you a beggar; you must become a son again before you can claim your birthright. Therefore, demand to be a son before you demand anything else. First establish your identity with God, as Jesus did, by realizing, in the joy of meditation, "I and my Father are one." Do not beseech Him like a beggar, but unite your ignorance-separated soul with God by constantly remaining identified with the ever-new Bliss within you.

After you have reestablished your joyous contact with Bliss-God, you may offer your demands for health, prosperity, or wisdom through mental whispers.

6

You must not be discouraged because of ill health, poverty, or moral weakness. Remember, suffering and sin are only temporary grafts; in reality you are eternally a Child of God. Even if the world condemns you and casts you away, God will ever seek to find you and bring you back home. Never mind if you cannot see Him or hear His knock at the gate of your heart.

→7←

Solitude is the price of God-contact. Knowledge of the laws of tuning the body, mind, and soul radios to God is necessary. But since God is also above law, devotion is necessary to call His attention. The devotional call, if sincere, deep, and continuous, and if supplemented by sincere efforts at deep meditation, will bring a divine response. Devotional demand is greater than law, for it touches the heart of God and makes Him answer His naughty and good children alike. Love causes God to surrender Himself to the devotee.

Don't be like the baby who stops crying as soon as his mother gives him a toy, but cry unceasingly, like a naughty baby, throwing away all lures and toys of name, fame, power, and possessions, rending the heart of the Divine Mother; then you will find the answer to your prayers. Pray until you are absolutely sure of the divine contact; then claim your material, mental, and spiritual needs from the Most High as your divine birthright.

⟩8⟨

Meditation is complete relaxation, the only way to know God. You can do everything else but meditate, and you will never find that joy that comes when the thoughts are silent.

You may ask, "How can I be sure there is such a joy as you describe?" This is my testimony: If you practice meditation every day deeply and consistently, you will find ever-existing, ever-conscious, ever-new joy within you. With practice it will stay with you in activity and in silence alike, even in sleep. It is a joy that will constantly guide you to right action in everything and will respond to your prayers.

This again is my testimony: Having reached that joy, you will find that other desires become small in comparison. Your consciousness will expand. You will stand unshaken amidst pulverizing trials. The whole world will not be able to lure you to forsake that bliss. You will enjoy all of life in that bliss.

⟩9⟨

The joy that comes in meditation is proof of the existence of the ever-new joyous God. Oftentimes when sleep steals over me, I say, "Go away from me, you gross intoxicant; I do not want to lose this joy in your unconsciousness."

Your whole body changes when you practice meditation frequently, because when you really contact God, all things become harmonious; all things melt into an ocean of peace. But you have to practice the meditation techniques honestly, earnestly, consistently, and continually, in order to have the full consciousness of that supreme force.

→10←

You have forgotten that your kingdom is omnipresence. Look in a mirror and see what you have done to yourself. Age is nothing, but when you show age, that is bad. You must always be sparkling within, with infinite wit and light. God is twinkling behind your eyes, but you screen Him off. Remember, behind the darkness of closed eyes is the light of God. And that kingdom is yours. You are omnipresent. Your home is eternity.

→11←

If we meditate on our blessings, on what we have to be thankful for rather than upon the trials, ills, and worries that beset or disturb us, we shall begin to know God.

⇾12⇽

The more you feel peace in meditation, the nearer you are to God.

⇾13⇽

During deep meditation a very enjoyable state of peace is produced, but afterwards, the loud breath revives, rousing all material desires and distractions. The devotee should not be discouraged at this but should, by deeper meditation, learn to calm the breath and the senses.

Even if one cannot conquer the flesh, he must meditate just the same, for then he will be able to compare the lesser pleasures of the senses and the greater pleasures of the soul.

⇾14⇽

As long as a restless thought or a bodily motion remains, you cannot hear the Inner Voice, or see with the Inner Eye. In other words, God will not enter your temple. In an inwardly and outwardly still body temple, illuminated by devotion, love, and inspiration, God may be coaxed to come. Real intuition and real vision will be awakened.

→15←

It is necessary to sit upright. When you sit with your spine bent and lean over, the body seems to say you are ready to give up. You must sit as if you mean business.

A bent spine is the enemy of self-realization. Your mind is on the bent spine; your electric currents will be busy with the muscles and flesh, and you cannot concentrate upon God. Practice discipline over the body, and your mind will be free to lift your consciousness from the body to the Infinite.

→16←

During meditation, some people fall asleep. You must be wide-awake. If you have a spell of sleepiness, shake it off—tense the body all over, and sleep will disappear. Fresh air also keeps one awake.

→17←

Self-realization is like a tender seed. You must water it with meditation and grow a hedge around it so that worries, fears, and anger will not tear down the little plant.

Meditate and keep your mind constantly pointed toward the North Pole of God's consciousness. Be like the compass. No matter how it is turned, the little needle of attention goes back to the North Pole. And so should your consciousness. Be with God every minute. Enjoy everything with the Infinite and you will be happy in that consciousness.

→18←

The mind must manifest calmness. Where the worries and trials of everyday life are concerned, the mind must be like water, which does not retain any impression of the waves that play on its surface.

Through the practice of meditation, one can achieve complete calmness in the heart, lungs, and other inner organs. When the muscles and inner organs are freed from motion by relaxation, the decay or breaking down of bodily tissues is temporarily inhibited.

Enter into absolute silence every morning, and banish thoughts for several minutes each time. The more you meditate, the more you will realize that nothing else can give you that refined joy but the increasing joy of silence. That joy-contact in meditation is contact with God. Pray deeply with devotion, first for God's love, then for wisdom, happiness, health, prosperity, and then for the fulfillment of any specific legitimate wish.

⇢19⇠

The minutes are more important than the years. If you fill the minutes of your life with thoughts of God, you will find the years of your life automatically saturated with the consciousness of God.

Never think of tomorrow. Take care of today and all the tomorrows will be taken care of. Do not wait until tomorrow to meditate. Do not wait until tomorrow to be good. Be good now. Be calm now. It will be the turning point of your life.

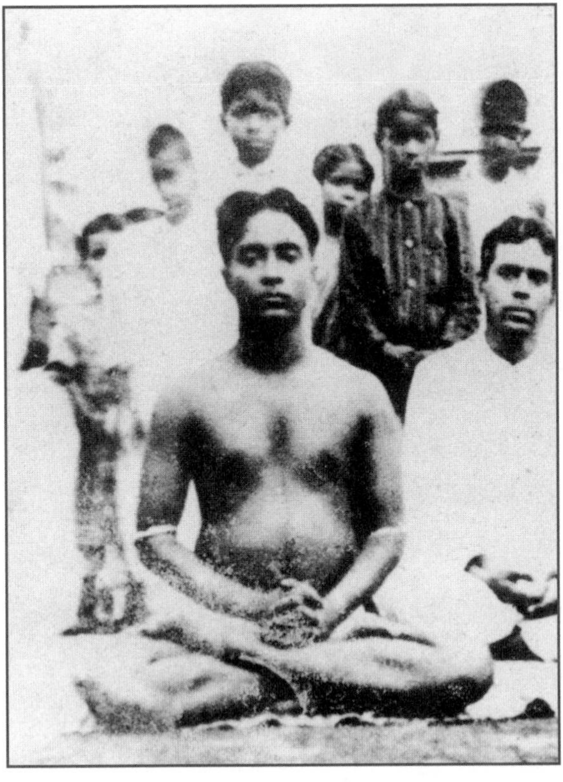

Chapter 9

Meditation Techniques

→1←

Practice the following exercise in the morning as soon as you awake, during the lunch hour, and also before going to bed: Lie on your back, relaxed and motionless. Do not think about time.

Offer a deep prayer of devotion to God until you feel that He has responded to you. Through the increase of your inner peace and inner satisfaction, know that God has heard you. Then, with eyes closed, exhale and, with breath out, concentrate your gaze and mind at the point between the eyebrows, mentally repeating twelve times: Om-Spirit-Christ, or Om-Spirit-Bliss. Then inhale.

Repeat the above exercise twelve or twenty-four times. Then, offer a deep heart's prayer to God until you feel the contact of God through ever-increasing peace.

The surest sign of the presence of God is a living, conscious peace filling you. The longer and more deeply you concentrate, the greater will be the increase of this peace, which is the language of God.

After you feel this deep peace within you, affirm, "Spirit and I are one. Spirit, manifest Thy wisdom fully through me." Or, "Spirit and I are one. Thou art my Father, I am Thy child. What Thou hast, I have. Give to me as Thy child all the real prosperity which belongs to me."

→2←

The following meditations will help the spiritual aspirant release his soul from confinement in the body to its eternal freedom in infinity.

- As soon as you wake, sit upright, look out of the open window into the vastness of the sky—or if you cannot see the sky from your window, mentally visualize it. Imagine your mind watching your body, the room, and the sky simultaneously. Meditate for a few minutes until you feel that you are the body, the room, and the sky. You can also practice this meditation in a beautiful outdoor setting, during the day or night.

- Sit upright and close your eyes. Imagine you are sitting on the center of the floor of your world-home, of which the sky is the roof. Visualize this world-home decorated with snow on the north and south poles, and inlaid with mountains, rivers, and pools of oceans filled with frothy wavelets. Behold the ferns of forests that bedeck your earthly house.

Now picture all your relative nations, races, families, and your loved ones gathered around you, playing the drama of life on the stage of time. Mentally say: "Hello, my white, brown, dark, and yellow-colored fathers, mothers, brothers, sisters, and friends." Try to feel all races as your own family and loved ones.

Mentally say: "Let us all bow to our One Father, God, Who made us all in His image. Let us bow to our grandparents, Adam and Eve, whose blood runs in all our veins. Let us thank God for putting us in our one big home of the earth; let us live happily and harmoniously and according to His will."

- Meditate with closed eyes. Mentally say, "I dissolve my body in darkness." Watch the limitless dark space of eternity spread above, beneath, in front, behind, within, and without—everywhere. Then, visualize a sealed rainbow balloon of light surrounding your body. This rubber balloon of light can never burst, no matter how you blow your luminous breath into it.

Exhale very slowly and visualize this balloon of light expanding with your luminous breath until it becomes big enough to contain star clusters, universes, and planetary and solar systems, including your earth and your body.

3

Sit upright with shoulder blades lightly drawn together, chest out, abdomen in, hands at the juncture of thighs and abdomen. Concentrate at the point between the eyebrows. Forget the body, the house, the earth, the sun and sky; forget flesh, thoughts, and feelings. Feel only the vastness within yourself.

Repeat to yourself, "I am Infinite, I am Infinite, I am Infinite." Go on mentally affirming this until you feel that you are beyond everything. Say, "I am timeless, I am spaceless, I am beyond body, thought, and speech; beyond matter and mind. I am Infinite, I am Infinite Blessedness." Meditate on that.

4

Concentrate at the point between the eyebrows. Expel the breath, inhale slowly through the nostrils, hold the breath, counting one to twelve and feeling all energy centering at the point between the eyebrows. Exhale slowly, and then inhale slowly through the nostrils, hold the breath, counting to twenty-five. Exhale slowly. Inhale slowly through the nostrils, hold the breath, counting to forty, feeling all energy at the point between the eyebrows. Exhale slowly. Now forget the breath and concentrate at the point between the eyebrows.

5

Imagine a ball of darkness. Feel that ball of darkness expanding to include your room, your city, your state. That ball of darkness is expanding farther to include the entire United States, all nations, the stars, Milky Way, and universes, until that ball of darkness includes the entire cosmos. Now imagine that ball of darkness is becoming light. Feel that that luminous ball of light is swallowing up everything. All space is a burning ball of flame, which now becomes a ball of unending happiness. You are that happiness. Meditate on that.

6

The *Hong-Sau* Technique of Concentration

You can practice this technique at any time. Wherever you are, sit erect with your spine straight, and deeply relax. Close your eyes (or fix their gaze, eyes half closed, at the point between the eyebrows). Now, with deep calmness, mentally watch your breath, *without controlling it, as it enters and exits the body*. As the breath enters, move the index finger of your right hand inward, toward the thumb, and mentally (without moving your tongue or lips) chant "*Hong*." As the breath exits, straighten the index finger, and mentally chant "*Sau*" (pronounced "saw"). (The purpose for moving the index finger is to become more effective in your concentration, and to differentiate the inhalation from the exhalation.)

Do not in any way control the breath mentally. Assume, rather, the calm attitude of a *silent observer,* watching the breath's natural flow as it enters and exits the body.

Practice this technique with great reverence and attention for at least ten minutes (to begin with). The longer your practice, the better. It will give you a deep sense of inner calmness, and will bring you at last to the realization that you are not the body, but the soul—superior to and independent of this material body.

For formal meditation, sit on a straight-backed, armless chair. Place a woolen blanket over the chair, covering the back and letting it run down beneath your feet. Face east. Sit erect, away from the back of the chair. Prepare yourself to practice *Hong-Sau* by first relaxing your body: inhale and tense the muscles of the whole body, throw out the breath and relax.

The *Hong-Sau* technique can also be practiced during leisure moments—such as sitting in a doctor's waiting room. Simply watch the breath, and as you do so, mentally chant "*Hong*" and "*Sau*," without moving the finger, closing the eyes, or gazing upward at the point between the eyebrows, or doing anything that might attract the attention of others around you.

The purpose of the *Hong-Sau* technique is to help you free your attention from outwardness, and to withdraw it from the senses, for breath is the cord that keeps the soul tied to the body. Man lives in an atmosphere of air, which he requires even as a fish requires water. By rising above the breath in breathlessness, man can enter the celestial realms of light, where the angels dwell. By dispassionately watching the breath coming in and going out, one's breathing naturally slows, calming at last the peace-disturbing activity of the heart, lungs, and diaphragm.

Consider for a moment this extraordinary fact: The heart pumps many tons of blood a day! It gets no rest even at night, when most of the other organs have a chance to suspend their activity at least partially. The most worked (and overworked) organ in the body is the heart. The *Hong-Sau* technique is a scientific method for resting the heart, thereby increasing longevity, and liberating a vast amount of Life Current, or energy, to be distributed over the whole body, renewing all the body cells and preventing their decay.

This marvelous, though simple, technique is one of India's greatest contributions to the world. It lengthens man's lifespan, and is a practical method for rising above body-consciousness and realizing oneself as the Immortal Spirit. The words, *Hong* and *Sau*, are a Sanskrit saying, given mantric power. The basic saying, *Aham saha*, means, "I—am He."

The Importance of Relaxation

In sleep, we experience sensory relaxation. Death is complete, though involuntary, relaxation of the spirit from the body. It comes after the arrest of the heart's action. By the *Hong-Sau* technique, one can reach the point of relaxing even the heart, and thereby rising above its compulsion to outwardness, experiencing death *consciously*, and eliminating one's sense of the mystery of death and the fear of dying. One can learn, indeed, to leave his body voluntarily and blissfully at death, rather than being thrown out of it forcefully, often as a complete surprise.

Inattention during practice of this technique can be soporific, producing sleep. Concentrated attention, on the other hand, brings to every body cell a tingling sense of divine life.

If you have the time, practice the technique longer—indeed, as long as you like. I myself, as a boy, used to practice it for seven hours at a time, and thereby achieved a deep state of breathless trance. Hold to the great calmness you feel during and after this practice. Cling to that peace as long as possible. Apply it in practical life situations, when dealing with people, when studying, when doing business, when thinking. And use it to help you practice self-control, when trying to rid yourself of some deep-seated, harmful mental or emotional habit. Whenever a situation demands it, recall to mind the calmness you've felt during and after the practice of this technique, and, reliving that state, meet the situation from that calm inner center, where your natural soul-intuition will ensure the best possible outcome.

Remember, deep intensity of concentration is necessary for the correct practice of this technique. This does not mean, however, that there should be any sense of strain. Practice the technique calmly, with relaxation—even with reverence—and feel in that calmness that you are placing yourself in readiness to listen to, and to become absorbed in, the Cosmic Vibration, *AUM. Hong-Sau* will help to put you in contact with the Great Spirit, who is present in you as your soul, and whose expression is vibration, the cause of that inner sound. Results will positively come, and deep calmness will be yours. Higher intuitions will come to you after prolonged practice, and you will find yourself in touch with the unexplored reservoir of divine power.

Do not be impatient. Keep on steadily. Incorporate this practice into your regular routine, making it as much a part of your day as eating, brushing your teeth and bathing, or sleeping. Supremely beneficial effects will pervade your whole mental and physical constitution.

As in everything else, the highest results cannot be attained in a day or even in days. Practice! Practice the technique, and apply to your daily needs the calmness it produces. Remember also, I speak from experience—not only my own, but that of centuries of meditation by the great yogis in my country. You, too, can have the same glorious experience as they, if you persevere in your practice.

Final, Important Point: Where to Concentrate?

Where should you focus your attention, while practicing this technique? On the breath, yes, but w*here* in the body?

Your attention, at first, may be on the pumping lungs and diaphragm. Concentrate first, then, on that physical movement. Gradually, as the mind grows calm, shift your attention from the body to the breath itself. Be aware of the breath where it enters the body, in the nostrils. As you grow calmer still, try to feel where, in the nostrils, the flow is strongest. At first it will be at the outer nostrils themselves, but as your concentration deepens try to feel the breath higher in the nose, and note where the flow seems strongest. As you grow still calmer, feel the breath where it enters the head, up by the point between the eyebrows—the actual seat of concentration in the body.

The origin of the breath lies in the astral body. Astral inhalation corresponds to an upward movement through what is known in the Yoga teachings as *ida*. Astral exhalation corresponds to a downward movement through the *pingala* nerve channel. These channels may be observed by those who eat fish as the two little nerves that run down the length of the spine.

An upward flow of energy through *ida* accompanies inhalation of the physical breath. And a downward flow through *pingala* accompanies physical exhalation. Astral breathing is accomplished by this upward and downward movement of energy. It is intrinsic to the reactive process. When the upward flow of energy is stronger, a positive reaction is indicated, and the same is true with deliberate physical inhalation. When the movement is more strongly downward (or when the physical exhalation is stronger than the inhalation), it comes out as a sigh, and indicates a feeling of rejection. When the inhalation is longer than the exhalation, it is an indication of positive reaction—even one of excitement. When the exhalation is longer, there is a corresponding withdrawal into oneself. In sleep, the exhalation is twice as long as the inhalation. When inhalation and exhalation are equal in duration, there is inner equanimity.

→7←

In doing the *Hong-Sau* technique, do not force the breath in and out. Breathe naturally, but watch the course of the incoming and outgoing breath, mentally chanting *Hong* and *Sau*. If the breath stops naturally after the inhalation or the exhalation, wait until it flows again of itself. Enjoy the pauses between the breaths. Let the mental chant follow the natural desire of the breath to flow in and out.

Remember that the purpose of this practice is to increase naturally the intervals when the breath does not flow. If the breath goes in of itself and does not flow out immediately, enjoy the state of breathlessness. When it comes out again, say *Sau*. If the breath goes out and stays out, enjoy that state of breathlessness, until the breath wants to flow in again.

Concentrate upon the intervals when the breath does not flow, without forcing this quiet breathless state.

By watching the breath, you destroy the identification of the soul with the body and breath. By watching the breath, you separate your ego from it and know that your body exists only partially by breath.

By watching the breath, breathing becomes rhythmic and calm. By watching the breath calmly, both the breath and the mind become calm. A calm mind and breath quiet the motion of the heart, diaphragm, and lungs.

When the motion is simultaneously removed from the muscles by relaxation and by casting out the breath, and from the inner organs, heart, lungs, diaphragm, and so on, then the Life Energy, which every day pumps many tons of blood through the heart, retires to the spine and becomes distributed in the billions of body cells. This energy electrifies the cells and prevents their decay. In such a state the cells do not require oxygen or food chemicals to sustain life. When decay is removed from outer and inner organs, the venous blood does not need to be sent to the heart to be pumped into the lungs to be purified by the incoming oxygen in the breath.

Because of removing impurities from the venous blood, and removing outer motion and inner motion by watching the breath, the technique frees one from the necessity of living by the human breath and the necessity of heart action.

When man is free from heart action and breath and lives by "the Word of God" (Cosmic Energy), his body will be charged with Cosmic Energy, and it will not need to depend upon outer sources of life (food, water, and breath). This brings greater longevity.

8

During meditation the yogi feels the power of concentration in the will center at the point between the eyebrows, and also experiences a feeling of complete peace throughout his body. When he wants to scour from the brain cells the seeds of past failure or sickness, he must direct that peace-and-concentration power to be felt in the entire brain. In this way the brain cells become impregnated with peace and power, and their hereditary chemical and psychological composition is altered.

9

Every night when you sit to meditate, pray to God unceasingly. Cry as you once cried to your mother or father, "Where are You? You made me. You are in the flowers, in the moon, and in the stars. Must You remain secret? Come to me. You must. You must." With the intellect and the love of your heart, tear at the veils of silence. With the rod of devotion churn the ether, and it shall produce God.

Chapter *10*

Live Your True Potential

→1←

The wakeful soul desires less and less, and finds his soul a sea of contentment. In noble desires, such as the desire to help others, however, the soul does not lose his peace, but rather finds his joy enlarged with the joys of those he has helped.

Do not squander your soul's peace by constantly running after small desires. When the vast reservoir of inner peace is let out through the channels of little desires, those waters of contentment are lost on the soil of material perceptions.

→2←

Cultivate emotional poise. To overcome restlessness, start with the determination to do each piece of work in its turn without unnecessary fuss, without burdening your mind with useless queries. Limit your thoughts to the task at hand. Dismiss the task just finished and allow the next task to take its turn.

A Spiritual Pledge Offered by Yogananda

I will concentrate on the teachings and will be loyal to the faithful daily practice of the techniques.

I will have a little temple in my room wherever I am (a closet or even a screened-off corner).

I will consider myself the minister of my temple, to correct myself and teach the audience (consisting of my diverse, untrained thoughts and feelings) so that I may be an ideal example and thereby be of real service to my fellow beings.

I will help others to the best of my ability every day, materially, mentally, and spiritually.

I will endeavor to live by the following Moral and Spiritual Rules:

I will not judge others—only myself.

I will strictly refuse to hear or read unkind discussions of others.

I will try to be efficient in everything—neither passively depending on God nor egotistically claiming the credit for myself when I have accomplished anything.

I will make myself successful through my own efforts and the power of God in me.

I will love all temples and churches as my Father's home, but I will be loyal to these teachings. I will try to support in whatever way I can my local Center.

3

Under all circumstances you must be calm and self-possessed. Even if storms of trials come, you must be able to calmly steer the ship of concentration to the shores of blessedness.

The ordinary person is influenced by his environment. The man of concentration shapes his own life. He plans his day and, at the end of the day, finds his plans completed and himself nearer to God and to his goal.

You must blame no one but yourself for your troubles. Every morning, make up your mind that you are going to be kind to your friends and enemies alike; to meditate more deeply than the day before; to know something about good books, and so forth. Analyze yourself and find out whether you have been progressing or not. You must not lead a stagnant existence. Every day, spur yourself on to greater achievements.

4

Be sure that what you want is right for you to have, then use all the forces of your will power to accomplish your object, always keeping your mind on God. No other desire must be in your heart but to know God; then all things will come to you.

→5←

To create dynamic will power, determine to do all the things in life you thought you couldn't do, and devote your entire will power to accomplishing one thing at a time. Be sure that you have made a good selection, then refuse to submit to failure. Use your will power to perfect yourself in this life. You must depend more and more upon the mind, because mind is the creator of your body and your circumstances.

→6←

Henceforth, make up your mind to perform your interesting duties with your whole heart and your uninteresting duties with deep attention.

Exclude every distracting thought that arises in you when you are mentally concentrating on an important problem. Most people are always thinking of an entirely different matter when they are doing important duties. Some businessmen are neither good moneymakers nor successful husbands, because when they are in their offices they are brooding over troubles with their wives, and when they are at home they ruminate on business troubles.

Concentrate upon one thing at a time. Your concentration

becomes super-concentration when you increase it to limitless accomplishing power by combining with it God's power.

→7←

Meditate regularly for half an hour every morning and half an hour before going to bed at night. Then sit quietly after meditation, feeling a calm peace. *The feeling that makes you enjoy peace during or after deep meditation is called "intuition."* If you keep exercising this power daily, it will grow and be ready to help you.

Whenever you want to solve a problem intuitively, first go into deep meditation or silence. Don't think of your problem during meditation. Meditate until you feel a sense of calmness that fills the inner recesses of your body; your breath becomes calm and quiet. Then concentrate simultaneously at the point between the eyebrows and the heart. Ask God to direct your intuition, so that you may know what to do about your problem.

Intuition is developed by:

- exercising common sense;
- daily introspection and analysis;
- depth of thought and concentrated activity;

- calmness; and
- holding onto the calm aftereffects of meditation.

You must concentrate upon increasing the receptive quality of your intuition. The infinite seat of all knowledge lies within you. With an awakened brain, you will understand all things.

→8←

The yogi always tries to keep his meditation-born peace enthroned in his mind, in every activity and in all dealings with others. If you are a god of peace after meditation, and suddenly change into a devil of disharmony at the drop of a hat, then your meditations are of little use. Meditation reminds you of your forgotten peace-nature, and with it you subdue your mortally acquired mental disquietude.

→9←

Keep your concentration on the aftereffects of meditation every minute of your existence, and do not neutralize that peace with disturbing thoughts.

If you throw a bag of mustard seeds on the ground, it is hard to gather the seeds back into the bag. If by recklessness you let loose the bag of concentration, all the thoughts like mustard seeds will scatter and it will be hard to get them together again. By collecting the thoughts together and grinding them with the power of concentration, you can bring out the oil of Self-realization.

→10←

Do not seek recognition. Seek to please God. People will then seek you, because they will feel that quality in you which reflects God. Carry God as the torch in your heart into all the pathways of your daily life. You will never stand alone and friendless if you consciously contact God. All else may fail you and fall away, but He will never fail you.

Give God a chance to tempt you with His love. Then nothing else can ever tempt and overcome you. You find material temptation charming only because you do not yet know the joys of soul happiness. You can compare only after you have experienced both.

Test your habits and see if they are controlling you. Show them that you have dominion. Let nothing interfere with your happiness. You will never be satisfied and free from misery until you know God and abide in Him; your soul must find the Whole to be complete.

Remember that virtue always triumphs in the end, even though it may take more than one lifetime. Never become discouraged through suffering and loss. Through your sufferings, learn to sympathize with others and to feel yourself in all. You will enter into your true kingdom at last, in happiness beyond expectation.

→11←

Do not expect to be successful in all your attempts the first time. Some ventures may fail, but others will be successful. With concentrated energy you must approach your nearest duty and do your utmost to accomplish whatever is needed.

In order to align yourself with God's abundance, you must eradicate forever from your mind all thought of poverty or lack. Universal mind is perfect, it knows no lack; and to align yourself with that never-failing Supply House you must create a consciousness of abundance, even if you do not know where the next dollar will come from.

Since all business, directly or indirectly, is connected with God's laws, bring God's conscious presence into your mind through meditation, in order to solve your God-given problems.

→12←

Always dwell on the thought of your innate perfection in God. Gold is still gold, though it lay buried under the accumulated filth of ages.

→13←

Let your supreme goal be to make others happy in order to gain happiness for yourself. Never think that you are acting unselfishly. Always think that you are doing things for your own pleasure, that you find your pleasure in making others happy.

→14←

God loves you just as much as He loves Krishna, Jesus, and the other great masters. You are a drop of the same ocean of Spirit. For the ocean is made up of all its drops. You are a part of God. You were given your importance by the Lord Himself. You are His very own.

→15←

Just as the pianist is always thinking of her music, so the lover of God is always thinking of God. That joy feeds the brain, the heart, and the soul. That ever-new joy is God.

⇾16⇽

The voice of the Infinite is strong and powerful, and when that power surcharges your body, all wrong vibrations vanish. When you feel the Eternal Power talking through your voice, through your silence, through your actions, through your reason, then you know you have something that will last beyond the grave.

⇾17⇽

You have been in a state of hallucination thinking that you are a mortal, struggling and suffering. Through meditation you come in contact with your Real Self and forget what you thought you were.

Every day you should sit quietly and say: "I am not the earth, nor the sky. No birth nor death have I. Father, mother, have I none; I am infinite Happiness." If you repeat this often and think about it day and night, you will realize what you really are. Only those who meditate realize that in the superconscious mind is a land of eternal happiness.

God is moving nearer and nearer to you the more deeply you meditate. The peace of meditation is the language and embracing comfort of God. Find God on the throne of peace within you first, and you will find Him in all the noble pursuits of life: in true friends, in the beauty of Nature, in good books, in good thoughts, in noble aspirations.

Nothing except God can satisfy you or completely wipe away your miseries. Your soul, a separate Part, must find the Whole to be complete. Your satisfaction must find perfect satisfaction in God; your knowledge must quench its thirst by drinking the wisdom of God; your peace can only be complete with the peace of God; your existence can only be immortal with the immortality of God; your consciousness can only be unceasing when attached to cosmic consciousness; your joy can be unending, ever entertaining, when combined with the joy of God.

→18←

The little centuries of human years are but days, nay, a few hours, in God's consciousness. Wake up! Arise from dreams of littleness to the realization of the vastness within you. You are dreaming that you are a big bee, buzzing around the poisoned honey of blossoming sense-lures.

Come, I will show you that you are the eternal fire, drinking with countless mouths the nectar-bliss hidden in the honeycombs of all hearts and all things. Feed no more your human habits with delusive human actions. Instead, meditate constantly and love God all the time, so that your own omnipresent nature may be revived in your consciousness, displacing body-bound, sense-bound beliefs and habits.

Drink the nectar of God-love in all hearts. Use every heart as your own wine cup to drink the ambrosia of God-love. Do not drink divine love from one heart only, but drink from all hearts the love of God alone.

Learn to love God as the joy felt in meditation. Victory is very near. Choose only good paths before you start hastily racing. Think of God as you start on the path of your material or spiritual duty. Think of God with each footfall of your advancing feet on your path.

By your own will, choose good food. Then think of God before you eat that food; think of God while you are eating it; and when eating is finished, think of God.

Invoke God as power in the temple of consciousness during the day. Let every word and action be tinged with God-love intoxication. Talk and act sensibly, yet be drunk with God, and let every action of daily life be a temple of God's memory. Perform every action to please Him, and in the shrine of every action, every thought, God will glisten.

Carry your love of God deep into your heart before you go to sleep, so that when you dream, you may dream of Him resting on the altar of sleep as Krishna, Christ, Peace, or Bliss. When you go to sleep, God embraces you to His bosom as peace and joy. You are sleeping locked in His arms of tranquility. So, before you fall asleep, think that you are going to embrace Him as peace in sleep and dreams.

Enthrone peace and joy in your heart. Feel joy no matter whom you meet or what you do. If you can do this, though the universe shatters to nothingness or your body is torn by trials, you will find Him dancing in your memory always.

Hold on to your spiritual treasure of joy. Culture it by instilling it in other hearts. Never surrender your joy to the robbers of worry or selfishness. Hold on to joy, no matter if death frowns at your door, or your own subconscious mind tells you, "All is lost."

Drown all noises with the silence of your invincible joy, and you will feel God reigning on the altar of every thought and feeling. You will find that evil and misery were your own dream creations. You slept and dreamt a nightmare of evil; you wake in God and feel only joy and virtue existing everywhere.

Appendix

Practice the Techniques in This Book

Dear Reader,

In this book Yogananda offers many life-transforming techniques. You can use the following exercises throughout the day, to keep your consciousness high and expansive. If you do so, your life will be uplifted and blessed by inner joy.

The references are given by chapter and quotation number (Chapter: Quotation number).

Affirmation, 3:6, 6:1–7, 6:11

Attention, 5:7, 10:2, 10:7

Focus on goodness, 5:3, 5:9

How to overcome
- Fear, 4:7
- Inferiority or superiority complexes, 4:6
- Nervousness, 4:10
- Self-pity, 4:3–4

How to overcome
- Temptation, 2:4–5
- Worry, 4:8–9

Intuition, 10:8

Love God, 3:10–12, 10:19

Meditation techniques, 8:11, all of Chapter 9, 10:18

Prayer, 6:11, 7:2, 8:3, 8:5

Spiritual Pledge, 10:3

Index

About the Author

Paramhansa Yogananda

"As a bright light shining in the midst of darkness, so was Yogananda's presence in this world. Such a great soul comes on earth only rarely, when there is a real need among men."

—The Shankaracharya of Kanchipuram

Born in India in 1893, Paramhansa Yogananda was trained from his early years to bring India's ancient science of Self-realization to the West. In 1920 he moved to the United States to begin what was to develop into a worldwide work touching millions of lives. Americans were hungry for India's spiritual teachings, and for the liberating techniques of yoga.

In 1946 he published what has become a spiritual classic and one of the best-loved books of the twentieth century, *Autobiography of a Yogi*. In addition, Yogananda established headquarters for a worldwide work, wrote a number of books and study courses, gave lectures to thousands in most major cities across the United States, wrote music and poetry, and trained disciples. He was invited to the White House by Calvin Coolidge, and he initiated Mahatma Gandhi into Kriya Yoga, his most advanced meditation technique.

Yogananda's message to the West highlighted the unity of all religions, and the importance of love for God combined with scientific techniques of meditation.

Ananda Sangha Worldwide

Ananda Sangha is a fellowship of kindred souls following the teachings of Paramhansa Yogananda. The Sangha embraces the search for higher consciousness through the practice of meditation, and through the ideal of service to others in their quest for Self-realization. Approximately ten thousand spiritual seekers are affiliated with Ananda Sangha throughout the world.

Founded in 1968 by Swami Kriyananda, a direct disciple of Paramhansa Yogananda, Ananda includes seven communities in the United States, Europe, and in India. Worldwide, about one thousand devotees live in these spiritual communities, which are based on Yogananda's ideals of "plain living and high thinking."

Swami Kriyananda lived with his guru during the last four years of the Master's life, and continued to serve his organization for another ten years, bringing the teachings of Kriya Yoga and Self-realization to audiences in the United States, Europe, Australia, and, from 1958–1962, India. In 1968, together with a small group of close friends and students, he founded the first "world-brotherhood community" in the foothills of the Sierra Nevada Mountains in northeastern California. Initially a meditation retreat center located on sixty-seven acres of forested land, Ananda World-Brotherhood Community today encompasses one thousand acres where about 250 people live a dynamic, fulfilling life based on the principles and practices of spiritual, mental, and physical development, cooperation, respect, and divine friendship.

At this printing, after forty years of existence, Ananda is one of the most successful networks of intentional communities in the world. Urban communities have been developed in Palo Alto and Sacramento, California; Portland, Oregon; and Seattle, Washington. In Europe, near Assisi, Italy, a spiritual retreat and community was established in 1983, where today nearly one hundred residents from eight countries live. And in India, new communities have been founded in Gurgaon (near New Delhi) and in Pune.

The Expanding Light

We are visited by over two thousand people each year. Offering a varied, year-round schedule of classes and workshops on yoga, meditation, spiritual practices, yoga and meditation teacher training, and personal renewal retreats, The Expanding Light welcomes seekers from all backgrounds. Here you will find a loving, accepting environment, ideal for personal growth and spiritual renewal.

We strive to create an ideal relaxing and supportive environment for people to explore their own spiritual growth. We share the nonsectarian meditation practices and yoga philosophy of Paramhansa Yogananda and his direct disciple, Ananda's founder, Swami Kriyananda. Yogananda called his path "Self-realization," and our goal is to help our guests tune in to their own higher Selves.

Guests at The Expanding Light can learn the four practices that comprise Yogananda's teachings of Kriya Yoga: the Energization Exercises, the *Hong Sau* technique of concentration, the AUM technique, and Kriya Yoga. The first two techniques are available for all guests; the second two are available to those interested in pursuing this path more deeply.

Crystal Clarity Publishers

When you're seeking a book on practical spiritual living, you want to know it's based on an authentic tradition of timeless teachings, and that it resonates with integrity. This is the goal of Crystal Clarity Publishers: to offer you books of practical wisdom filled with true spiritual principles that have not only been tested through the ages, but also through personal experience.

We publish only books that combine creative thinking, universal principles, and a timeless message. Crystal Clarity books will open doors to help you discover more fulfillment and joy by living and acting from the center of peace within you.

Crystal Clarity Publishers—recognized worldwide for its best-selling, original, unaltered edition of Paramhansa Yogananda's classic *Autobiography of a Yogi*—offers many additional resources to assist you in your spiritual journey, including over one hundred books, a wide variety of inspirational and relaxation music composed by Swami Kriyananda (Yogananda's direct disciple), and yoga and meditation DVDs.

For our online catalog, complete with secure ordering, please visit us on the web at:

www.crystalclarity.com

Crystal Clarity music and audiobooks are available on all the popular online download sites. Look for us on your favorite online music website.

To request a catalog, place an order for the products you read about in the Further Explorations section of this book, or to find out more information about us and our products, please contact us:

Contact Information for Ananda Sangha Worldwide

mail: 14618 Tyler Foote Road • Nevada City, CA 95959
phone: 530.478.7560
online: www.ananda.org / sanghainfo@ananda.org

Contact Information the Expanding Light

mail: 14618 Tyler Foote Road • Nevada City, CA 95959
phone: 800.346.5350
online: www.expandinglight.org / info@expandinglight.org

Contact Information for Crystal Clarity Publishers

mail: 14618 Tyler Foote Road • Nevada City, CA 95959
phone: 800.424.1055 *or* 530.478.7600
online: www.crystalclarity.com / clarity@crystalclarity.com

Further Explorations

If you are inspired by this book and would like to learn more about Yogananda's teachings, we offer many additional resources:

Crystal Clarity publishes the original 1946, unedited edition of Paramhansa Yogananda's spiritual masterpiece

Autobiography of a Yogi

Paramhansa Yogananda

One of the best-selling Eastern philosophy titles of all time, with millions of copies sold, this book was named one of the best and most influential books of the twentieth century. This highly prized reprinting of the original 1946 edition is the only one available free from textual changes made after Yogananda's death.

In this updated edition are bonus materials, including a last chapter that Yogananda wrote in 1951, without posthumous changes, the eulogy that Yogananda wrote for Gandhi, and a new foreword and afterword by Swami Kriyananda, one of Yogananda's close, direct disciples.

PRAISE FOR *Autobiography of a Yogi*

"In the original edition, published during Yogananda's life, one is more in contact with Yogananda himself." *—David Frawley, Director, American Institute of Vedic Studies, author of* Yoga and Ayurveda

ALSO AVAILABLE AS AN **UNABRIDGED AUDIBOOK IN MP3 FORMAT**

Crystal Clarity is also pleased to offer these two biographies of Paramhansa Yogananda by his direct disciple, Swami Kriyananda.

Paramhansa Yogananda

A Biography with Personal Reflections and Reminiscences

Swami Kriyananda

Taking up where Yogananda's celebrated *Autobiography of a Yogi* leaves off., this book will thrill the millions of readers of Yogananda's autobiography with scores of new stories from Yogananda's life—some charmingly human, some deeply inspiring, and many recounting miracles equal to those of the Bible. These stories are told from first-hand experience, and bring the Master alive unlike any other book ever written about him.

Now, Swami Kriyananda brilliantly puts to rest many misconceptions about his great guru, and reveals Yogananda's many-sided greatness. The author's profound grasp of the purpose of Yogananda's life, his inner nature, and his plans for the future are revelatory and sublime. Included is an insider's portrait of the great teacher's last years. More than a factual biography, this book also outlines the great master's key teachings.

Feel the power of Paramhansa Yogananda's divine consciousness and his impact on the world as presented with clarity and love by one of his few remaining direct disciples.

The New Path

My Life with Paramhansa Yogananda

Swami Kriyananda

This is the moving story of Kriyananda's years with Paramhansa Yogananda, India's emissary to the West and the first yoga master to spend the greater part of his life in America.

When Swami Kriyananda discovered *Autobiography of a Yogi* in 1948, he was totally new to Eastern teachings. This is a great advantage to the Western reader, since Kriyananda walks us along the yogic path as he discovers it from the moment of his initiation as a disciple of Yogananda. With winning honesty, humor, and deep insight, he shares his journey along the spiritual path through personal stories and experiences.

PRAISE FOR *The New Path*

"Reading *Autobiography of a Yogi* by Yogananda was a transformative experience for me and for millions of others. In *The New Path* . . . Swami Kriyananda carries on this great tradition. Highly recommended." *—Dean Ornish, MD, Founder and President, Preventative Medicine Research Institute, Clinical Professor of Medicine, University of California, San Francisco, author of* The Spectrum

"Required reading for every spiritual seeker. I heartily recommend it." — *Michael Toms, Founder, New Dimensions Media, and author of* An Open Life: Joseph Campbell in Conversation with Michael Toms

ALSO AVAILABLE AS AN **UNABRIDGED AUDIOBOOK IN MP3 FORMAT**

The Essence of Self-Realization

The Wisdom of Paramhansa Yogananda

Recorded, Compiled, & Edited by His Disciple, Swami Kriyananda

With nearly three hundred sayings rich with spiritual wisdom, this book is the fruit of a labor of love. A glance at the table of contents will convince the reader of the vast scope of this book. It offers as complete an explanation of life's true purpose, and of the way to achieve that purpose, as may be found anywhere.

"Self-realization is the knowing in all parts of body, mind, and soul that you are now in possession of the kingdom of God ... that God's omnipresence is your omnipresence; and that all that you need to do is improve your knowing."
–*Swami Kriyananda, from the book*

Conversations with Yogananda

Edited with commentary by Swami Kriyananda

This is an unparalleled, first-hand account of the teachings of Paramhansa Yogananda. Featuring nearly 500 never-before-released stories, sayings, and insights, this is an extensive, yet eminently accessible, fund of wisdom from one of the twentieth century's most famous yoga masters. Compiled and edited with commentary by Swami Kriyananda, one of Yogananda's closest direct disciples.

"This book is a treasure trove. If your goal is to grow spiritually, get a copy now." —*Richard Salva, author of* Walking with William of Normandy: A Paramhansa Yogananda Pilgrimage Guide

The Essence of the Bhagavad Gita

Explained by Paramhansa Yogananda

As Remembered by His Disciple, Swami Kriyananda

Rarely in a lifetime does a new spiritual classic appear that has the power to change people's lives and transform future generations. This is such a book.

This revelation of India's best-loved scripture approaches it from a fresh perspective, showing its deep allegorical meaning and its down-to-earth practicality. The themes presented are universal: how to achieve victory in life in union with the divine; how to prepare for life's "final exam," death, and what happens afterward; and, how to triumph over all pain and suffering.

PRAISE FOR *The Essence of the Bhagavad Gita*

"A brilliant text that will greatly enhance the spiritual life of every reader." *—Caroline Myss, author of* Anatomy of the Spirit *and* Sacred Contracts

"It is doubtful that there has been a more important spiritual writing in the last fifty years than this soul-stirring, monumental work. What a gift! What a treasure!" *—Neale Donald Walsch, author of* Conversations with God

"I loved reading this!" *—Fred Alan Wolf, Ph.D., physicist, aka Dr. Quantum, author of* Dr. Quantum's Little Book of Big Ideas *and* The Yoga of Time Travel

"It has the power to change your life." *—Bernie Siegel, MD, author of* 101 Exercises for the Soul *and* Love, Medicine and Miraclesl

ALSO AVAILABLE AS AN **UNABRIDGED AUDIOBOOK IN MP3 FORMAT** AND AS **PAPERBACK WITHOUT COMMENTARY**: *THE BHAGAVAD GITA*

Whispers from Eternity

Paramhansa Yogananda

Edited by His Disciple, Swami Kriyananda

Yogananda was not only a spiritual master, but a master poet, whose poems revealed the hidden divine presence behind even everyday things.

Open this book, pick a poem at random, and read it. Mentally repeat whatever phrase appeals to you. Within a short time, you will feel your consciousness transformed. This book has the power to rapidly accelerate your spiritual growth, and provides hundreds of delightful ways for you to begin your own conversation with God.

ALSO AVAILABLE AS AN **UNABRIDGED AUDIOBOOK IN MP3 FORMAT**

Energization Exercises

Paramhansa Yogananda, Swami Kriyananda. and others

The *Energization Exercises*, as taught in the Ananda Course in Self-Realization, are a wonderful system of exercises originated by Paramhansa Yogananda. Best learned at Ananda, they are also taught here in a variety of formats.

Based on ancient teachings and eternal realities, Yogananda explains that the whole physical universe, including man, is surrounded by, and made of cosmic energy. Through daily use of these exercises we can systematically recharge our bodies with greater energy and train our minds to understand the true source of that power.

AVAILABLE IN **DVD, BOOKLET, BOOK. AND INSTRUCTIONAL CD**

Crystal Clarity is also pleased to offer an important series of scriptural interpretations based on the teachings of Paramhansa Yogananda.

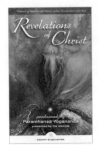

Revelations of Christ

Proclaimed by Paramhansa Yogananda,

Presented by His Disciple, Swami Kriyananda

Over the past years, our faith has been severely shaken by experiences such as the breakdown of church authority, discoveries of ancient texts that supposedly contradict long-held beliefs, and the sometimes outlandish historical analyses of Scripture by academics. Together, these forces have helped create confusion and uncertainty about the true teachings and meanings of Christ's life.

This soul-stirring book, presenting the teachings of Christ from the experience and perspective of Yogananda, finally offers the fresh understanding of Christ's teachings for which the world has been waiting, in a more reliable way than any other: by learning from those saints who have communed directly, in deep ecstasy, with Christ and God.

PRAISE FOR *Revelations of Christ*

"This is a great gift to humanity. It is a spiritual treasure to cherish and to pass on to children for generations. This remarkable and magnificent book brings us to the doorway of a deeper, richer embracing of Eternal Truth." —*Neale Donald Walsch, author of* Conversations with God

ALSO AVAILABLE AS AN **UNABRIDGED AUDIOBOOK IN MP3 FORMAT**

The Wisdom of Yogananda Series

This series features writings of Paramhansa Yogananda not available elsewhere. Included are writings from his earliest years in America, in an approachable, easy-to-read format and presented with minimal editing, to capture his expansive and compassionate wisdom, his sense of fun, and his practical spiritual guidance.

How to Be Happy All the Time

The Wisdom of Yogananda Series, Volume 1

Paramhansa Yogananda

Yogananda powerfully explains everything needed to lead a happier, more fulfilling life. Topics include: looking for happiness in the right places; choosing to be happy; tools and techniques for achieving happiness; sharing happiness with others; and balancing success and happiness.

"A fine starting point for reaching contentment." —*Bookwatch*

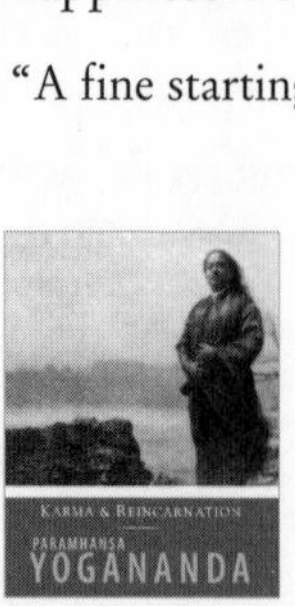

Karma and Reincarnation

The Wisdom of Yogananda Series, Volume 2

Paramhansa Yogananda

Yogananda reveals the truth behind karma, death, reincarnation, and the afterlife. With clarity and simplicity, he makes the mysterious understandable. Topics include: why we see a world of suffering and inequality; how to handle the challenges in our lives; what happens at death, and after death; and the origin and purpose of reincarnation.

Spiritual Relationships
The Wisdom of Yogananda Series, Volume 3
Paramhansa Yogananda

This book contains practical guidance and fresh insight on relationships of all types. Topics include: how to cure bad habits that can end true friendship; how to choose the right partner and create a lasting marriage; sex in marriage and how to conceive a spiritual child; problems that arise in marriage and what to do about them; the Universal Love behind all your relationships, and many more.

"[A] thoroughly 'user friendly' guide on how yoga principles can actually help relationships grow and thrive. Yogananda's keys to understanding yoga's underlying philosophy [teach] how to cure bad habits, expand love boundaries, and understand relationship problems."

—*James A. Cox, Chief Editor,* The Bookwatch

How to Be a Success
The Wisdom of Yogananda Series, Volume 4
Paramhansa Yogananda

This book includes the complete text of *The Attributes of Success*, the original booklet later published as *The Law of Success.* In addition, you will learn how to find your purpose in life, develop habits of success and eradicate habits of failure, develop your will power and magnetism, and thrive in the right job.

Winner of the 2011 International Book Award for the Best Self-Help Book of the Year

How to Have Courage, Calmness and Confidence

The Wisdom of Yogananda Series, Volume 5

Paramhansa Yogananda

Everyone can be courageous, calm, and confident, because these are qualities of the soul. Hypnotized with material thinking and desires, many of us have lost touch with our inner power. In this potent book of spiritual wisdom, Paramhansa Yogananda shares the most effective steps for reconnecting with your divine nature.

The Essence of Self-Realization

The Wisdom of Paramhansa Yogananda

Recorded, Compiled, & Edited by His Disciple, Swami Kriyananda

Paramhansa Yogananda, a foremost spiritual teacher of modern times, offers practical, wide-ranging, and fascinating suggestions on how to have more energy and to live a radiantly healthy life. The principles in this book promote physical health and all-round well-being, mental clarity, and ease and inspiration in your spiritual life.

Readers will discover • Priceless Energization Exercises for rejuvenating the body and mind • The art of conscious relaxation • Diet tips for health and beauty.

Music and Audiobooks

We offer many of our book titles in unabridged MP3 format audiobooks. To purchase these titles and to see more music and audiobook offerings, visit our website: www.crystalclarity.com. Or look for us in the popular online download sites.

Metaphysical Meditations

Swami Kriyananda

Kriyananda's soothing voice guides you in thirteen different meditations based on the soul-inspiring, mystical poetry of Yogananda. Each meditation is accompanied by beautiful classical music to help you quiet your thoughts and prepare for deep states of meditation. Includes a full recitation of Yogananda's poem "Samadhi." A great aid to the serious meditator, as well as to those just beginning their practice.

Relax: Meditations for Flute and Cello

Donald Walters

Featuring David Eby and Sharon Nani

This CD is specifically designed to slow respiration and heart rate, bringing listeners to their calm center. This recording features fifteen melodies for flute and cello, accompanied by harp, guitar, keyboard, and strings. Excellent for creating a calming atmosphere for work and home.

AUM: Mantra of Eternity

Swami Kriyananda

This recording features nearly seventy minutes of continuous vocal chanting of AUM, the Sanskrit word meaning peace and oneness of spirit, as extensively discussed by Yogananda in *Autobiography of a Yogi.* By attuning one's consciousness to this sound, one enters the stream of vibration that proceeded out of Spirit, and that emerges back into the Spirit at creation's end and at the end of the individual soul's cycle of outward wandering. By merging in AUM, liberation is attained.

OTHER TITLES IN THE MANTRA SERIES:

Gayatri Mantra ❁ *Mahamrityanjaya Mantra* ❁ *Maha Mantra*

Bliss Chants

Ananda Kirtan

Chanting focuses and lifts the mind to higher states of consciousness. *Bliss Chants* features chants written by Yogananda and his direct disciple, Swami Kriyananda. They're performed by Ananda Kirtan, a group of singers and musicians from Ananda, one of the world's most respected yoga communities. Chanting is accompanied by guitar, harmonium, kirtals, and tabla.

OTHER TITLES IN THE CHANT SERIES:

Divine Mother Chants ❁ *Power Chants* ❁ *Love Chants*

Peace Chants ❁ *Wisdom Chants* ❁ *Wellness Chants*

More Crystal Clarity Titles

Also from Crystal Clarity Publishers, some of our popular books

---